Advent, Christmas,

and Epiphany Services

D1495346

Other Abingdon Press books by F. Belton Joyner, Jr.

Life in the Fish Bowl

Ten Questions Every Pastor Fears*
*Answers Included

The Unofficial United Methodist Handbook (editor)

The Unofficial United Methodist Handbook for Pastors (editor)

JUST IN TIME!

ADVENT, CHRISTMAS, AND EPIPHANY SERVICES

F. Belton Joyner, Jr.

Abingdon Press
Nashville

JUST IN TIME!
ADVENT, CHRISTMAS, AND EPIPHANY SERVICES

Copyright © 2010 by Abingdon Press

This book is printed on acid-free paper.

Library of Congress Cataloging-in-Publication Data

Joyner, F. Belton.
    Advent, Christmas. and Epiphany services / F. Belton Joyner, Jr.
        p. cm. — (Just in time series)
    ISBN 978-1-4267-0680-6 (binding: book- pbk./trade pbk.. adhesive-perfect binding : alk. paper) 1. Advent. 2. Christmas. 3. Epiphany. 4. Worship programs. I. Title.
    BV40.J69 2010
    263'.912—dc22

                                                                    2009054428

10 11 12 13 14 15 16 17 18 19—10 9 8 7 6 5 4 3 2 1

MANUFACTURED IN THE UNITED STATES OF AMERICA

In memory of my parents,
who taught me how to worship God
by the way they loved God

CONTENTS

INTRODUCTION

This book reflects an awareness that our spiritual increase is dependent upon having good roots. We cannot expect fresh, green growth from a tree that does not in some way reach down into the soil of its beginnings. The first thing a brand new seed tries to do is to send out roots to connect with nourishment. Our Christian worship life needs to draw from our heritage as well as from our hopes. This book acknowledges the liturgical traditions of the church and, when plowing some new ground, still tries to honor "the one who brought us to the dance."

As I was working on this book, happily typing at my friendly desktop, my computer crashed. Boom! Just like that, all the documents I had saved were gone. Just like that, it was empty. Just like that, the things I had counted on were no more. When I realized how desperate I was to recover those data, I recognized in myself a primal need to stay in touch with where I have been. Although everything lost was not valuable, nevertheless the loss of the documents took away significant reminders of how I had been shaped, how I had responded to life, and how I existed as a product of relationships, sometimes even electronic relationships. All of this is to say that writing this Advent series is one way I try to stay linked to the expedition of the worshiping Christian faith community— to erase all that could change who I am and who I am called to be.

There is a common pattern in the seven chapters that prime the pump for Advent, Christmas Eve, Christmas Day, and Epiphany. (The chapter on seasonal funerals takes a different tack.)

This is that pattern:

DAY IN THE CHURCH YEAR

The heading for each chapter is the day in the church year for which this material might be helpful. Most of these days fall on a

Sunday, but Christmas Eve and Christmas Day services most likely come on a weekday. If you have either a Christmas Eve service or a Christmas Day service, you certainly may look at the sets of suggestions to see what rings true for your situation.

The Sundays during the Advent season are considered part of the Advent cycle (thus "Sundays *of Advent*"), unlike the Sundays that occur during the Lenten cycle, when Sunday is not part of Lent (thus "Sundays *in Lent*").

TITLE

Each chapter has a "teaser title." The "unlikely" theme is simply a prompt to help us recall that God's ways are not our ways and God's thoughts are not our thoughts. Often I think I can do better than God, but so far that has not proved to be the case.

QUESTION

This question is just to get the juices flowing.

A THOUGHT

In my first draft I called this section "an answer," but I discovered that some of my mumblings were not really solutions so much as a continuation of the question process. I tend to want to move too quickly to the answer without lingering in the refreshing waters of wonder, without waiting for further revelation from the living God. This heading ("A Thought") seems a bit less presumptuous.

SCRIPTURE

Some persons will note immediately that these scripture lessons are not from any lectionary cycle. That is intentional. There are already numbers of resources that open the doors for preachers who follow the lectionary. My typical preaching pattern is to follow the lectionary. Nevertheless, the wonderful good news of the season is that the story does not change and therein lies a comfort and a danger. The comfort is in the knowledge of the renewing cycle of God's love; the danger is that familiarity will breed boredom.

If you are a lectionary preacher, you still might find some energy in these services that grow out of non-lectionary texts. You might leave the lectionary for one Sunday and not for the others. If you are not one who follows the lectionary, consider these scriptures as yet another way to approach the season (or, more appropriately, to let God's season approach us!).

The texts are from the New Revised Standard Version.

CALL TO WORSHIP

Rather than using the "leader/people" format for these responsive readings, I use "One Voice" and "All Voices." Consider the possibility of having a different person read each time there is "One Voice." In some settings, an echo reading would be effective: the first time, for example, One Voice could be from the back of the worship space and the second time One Voice could come from the front of the space. Of course (and I checked the rules on this), there is nothing that says you cannot lead the whole thing yourself.

PASTORAL PRAYER

You might prefer to label this "congregational prayer" or "the church at prayer." In corporate worship, the pastor is praying on behalf of the people; "a pastoral prayer" is more than letting the people eavesdrop on the pastor's personal prayer. It is a prayer of all the people, articulated by one. As you look at these prayers, you might find a phrase that captures something you have wanted to say. Grab that phrase and toss out the rest, as you choose.

SOME INGREDIENTS TO STIR INTO THE SERMON POT

This is the longest section in each chapter. You will note quickly that this material is not a ready-made sermon. Here you will find some exploration of the text, exegetical work, and illustrations. And, truth to tell, occasionally my preacher mode kicks in and I begin writing the sermon I might preach. My hope is that you will use this portion of the chapter as a way of rebooting your own preaching computer, getting someone else's look at a text, and visiting someone else's struggle to let the text rub against daily life. These are indeed not mini (nor maxi) sermons. This section does just what its heading implies: offers some things you might want to consider as God leads you in your own sermon preparation. The title at the start of each reflection is offered as one way to pique congregational interest in order to prevent congregational napping!

A TIME WITH YOUNG DISCIPLES

This portion of the service goes by a variety of names: Time with Children, Children's Sermon, Message for Children, or Let Me Talk to the Adults in the Guise of Talking to the Children. If this practice is standard in your setting, you already know that careful attention must be paid to the age-appropriateness of what you do and say. It might be useful for children to know what "Eschatalogical Hermeneutic" means, but it is not likely that they have receptors to receive the wisdom I might expound on the subject. It is a delicate balance between talking down to the children ("Now, boys and girls, what do I have in my hand?"—pause for answer—"Wow! Yes! You are smart! You are exactly right. It is a book!") and going way over the heads of the children ("Now I want you to remember all next week what 'epiphanically oriented' means").

HYMNS

Singing together gives the church the heartbeat of the rhythm of faith. In this segment of the chapter, I have wanted to help you expand on the way in which hymn singing is done. These proposals can be applied in any worship services.

Some of the references may be to hymnals that are different from the one you have on hand. If so, rummage in your hymnal to see if you can "translate" these thoughts to your songbook. Whether your singing comes off a projection screen or from a printed page, it can come from the heart and head of the gathered flock.

ADVENT WREATH

Here are litanies that can be used throughout the season of Advent/Christmas, plus a suggestion for a replacement for the wreath on Epiphany Sunday. Note the hints as to whom to invite to light the candles. While practice does not always make perfect, it does cut down on embarrassment and distraction.

HAVE YOU THOUGHT OF DOING THIS?

The heading for the section says it all. (You know how it can be with preachers: after saying, "It goes without saying," we go ahead and say it!) These might prime your planning pump. Share these notions with your church council or a planning team.

Variations on the theme are acceptable! Although I thought of hiring investigators to go all over the country to make sure you were following my program suggestions to the nth degree, I decided that was too expensive, so have at it!

In fact, that is about what I want to say as my closing word: Have at it!

Jesus: The Unlikely Image of God

Question: What picture comes to mind when you think of God?
A Thought: Not humankind, but Jesus Christ is the perfect image of God.

Scripture: Genesis 1:26-27

Then God said, "Let us make humankind in our image, according to our likeness; and let them have dominion over the fish of the sea, and over the birds of the air, and over the cattle, and over all the wild animals of the earth, and over every creeping thing that creeps upon the earth."

So God created humankind in his image,
in the image of God he created them;
male and female he created them.

Colossians 1:15-17

He is the image of the invisible God, the firstborn of all creation; for in him all things in heaven and on earth were created, things visible and invisible, whether thrones or dominions or rulers or powers—all things have been created through him and for him. He himself is before all things, and in him all things hold together.

Call to Worship
One Voice: And God said, "Let us make humankind in our image."

1

All Voices: **We come to worship our Creator.**
One Voice: And God created humankind in the image of God, all humankind.
All Voices: **So we gather with brothers and with sisters, these here and those beyond this space.**
One Voice: And when that image of God was broken
All Voices: **God came in full visibility, to show and to restore that perfect image.**
One Voice: God came in Jesus Christ.
All Voices: **God came in Jesus Christ.**
One Voice: Born to set the people free!
All Voices: **Amen! Amen! Amen!**

Pastoral Prayer   12/29/20

O God, who has come and yet comes again, we are grateful for the ways in which you break into our lives. You bring the possibilities of joy in the midst of our despair. You offer the gift of community in the midst of our lonely places. You show us what tomorrow is meant to be in the midst of our complacency.

You have made us in your image, but we confess that what we see in the mirror of our lives does not look much like you, like your love, like your justice, like your peace. You live in the unbroken Trinity—Father, Son, and Holy Spirit—and we tarry in relationships that are shattered, neighbor divided against neighbor, nations torn from one another, and even sharp words we exchange with those closest to us.

In this season of looking at the birth of your Son, bring new birth into our hearts. Forgive the shadows we have put in front of your light and let the winds of your Spirit blow away the clouds that block others from seeing you in our lives.

(Here the one leading the prayer may include confessions, petitions, intercessions, and thanksgivings appropriate to the community.)

Hear the prayer we offer in the name and spirit of the One who shows you perfectly, even Jesus Christ, who taught us to pray, "Our Father . . ."

Some Ingredients to Stir into the Sermon Pot

Just John and Jane

If you were going to write a story that told the truth about all of humankind, what would you name the main characters? What names would you choose to represent all of us? When writing in North American English, persons will often use "John Doe" or "Jane Doe" to stand for the average, ordinary citizen. A politician who is considering a policy change might ask: "What would John and Jane Doe think about this? How will this new policy affect Jane Doe and John Doe?"

The writer of the first chapter of Genesis was inspired to name the pivotal characters of the account in such a way that readers would know that this story is indeed the story of John and Jane Doe. It is the story of all of us.

We know these central figures as Adam and Eve. The name Adam means human being. The name Eve means life giver. That's a pretty good clue that the creation account in Genesis is about you and me! In fact, *ha'adham* (recognize "Adam" in that Hebrew word?) is usually translated simply "humankind" or "man," no doubt a teasing way of remembering that God created us out of dust (Genesis 2:7). The Hebrew word for "dust of the earth, clay" is *ha'adhamah*. (Okay. Maybe it was funnier in ancient times to compare *ha'adham* and *ha'adhamah*. While this humor is not exactly a thigh slapper, it does keep us from getting concerned about Adam's shoe size and favorite color. This is not just the story of one person; it is the story of all persons!)

Eve gets named "Eve" (Genesis 3:20) because she is "the mother of all living." That's what the name means. Now, the writer of these verses has gone to meddling! I had a little wiggle room until now. As long as I can remain convinced that Eve was back then and I am now, then I can nudge her story into a kind of antique irrelevance. But, good grief, the scripture has sneaked up and captured me. If Adam is "humankind" and Eve is "the mother of all living," where can I go to hide from this story? It is clearly my story. And it is clearly your story. This ups the ante a little bit! So, what is our story? I might ask: "What do I learn about me from the story of Adam and Eve?"

I have two sisters. I was born in James Walker Memorial Hospital in Wilmington, North Carolina. I graduated from Siler City High School. I ran track when I was in college. Twice I have been an organizing pastor for new congregations. Toni and I (married for fifty years) have one son, one daughter-in-law, and three grandsons. We live out in the country surrounded by hardwood trees and venturesome deer. What else would you like to know?

Oops! You have caught me stalling, not quite ready to face the truth about me that shows up in the Genesis account. (I don't usually put "tell me the truth" on my hints for Christmas gifts.) Let's start at the beginning.

You and I are part of God's created order. The earth, the environment, the waters, the vegetation, the animals, light, dark— these are all gifts of God's creative initiative. Although my stomach is not fully convinced that God created asparagus, the biblical witness is that what God created was good (Genesis 1:4, 10, 12, 18, 21, 25). There was a whole lot of good going on! (The word translated as *good* means *suited to its purpose*.) So far, so good.

Maybe God should have stopped at that. Have you ever watched a football team successfully run a particular play, time after time? "Braxton fades back to pass; Riley is free again down that right sideline. And Braxton hits him in full stride! Another first down! That play has been working all day." But one time too many and on the next try: "Interception! Interception!" And what has been money in the bank has become a painful withdrawal. Going to the well too many times can mean a dry well.

Maybe God should have stopped at the creating business before he came to us! Perhaps like the man who said "I must have money in the bank because I still have blank checks," God looks at the earth he has created and says, "I still have more I can do." Should God have gone that next step? What would God's creation of beauty and purpose have been like if humankind had not been created?

4

James Weldon Johnson (1871–1938) described what God did next:

And God stepped out on space,
And He looked around and said,
"I'm lonely—
I'll make me a world."

And far as the eye of God could see
Darkness covered everything,
Blacker than a hundred midnights
Down in a cypress swamp.

Then God smiled,
And the light broke,
And the darkness rolled up on one side,
And the light stood shining on the other,
And God said, *"That's good!"*

Then God reached out and took the light in His hands,
And God rolled the light around in His hands
Until He made the sun;
And He set that sun a-blazing in the heavens.
And the light that was left from making the sun
God gathered up in a shining ball
And flung it against the darkness,
Spangling the night with the moon and stars.
Then down between
The darkness and the light
He hurled the world;
And God said, *"That's good!"*

Then God himself stepped down—
And the sun was on His right hand,
And the moon was on His left;
The stars were clustered about His head,
And the earth was under His feet.
And God walked, and where he trod
His footsteps hollowed the valleys out
And bulged the mountains up.

Then He stopped and looked and saw
That the earth was hot and barren.
So God stepped over to the edge of the world
And He spat out the seven seas;
He batted His eyes, and the lightnings flashed;
He clapped His hands, and the thunders rolled;
And the waters above the earth came down,
The cooling waters came down.

Then the green grass sprouted,
And the little red flowers blossomed,
The pine tree pointed his finger to the sky,
And the oak spread out his arms,
The lakes cuddled down in the hollows of the ground,
And the rivers ran down to the sea;
And God smiled again,
And the rainbow appeared,
And curled itself around His shoulder.

Then God raised His arm and He waved His hand
Over the sea and over the land,
And he said, *"Bring forth! Bring forth!"*
And quicker than God could drop His hand,
Fishes and fowls
And beasts and birds
Swam the rivers and the seas,
Roamed the forests and the woods,
And split the air with their wings.
And God said, *"That's good!"*

Then God walked around,
And God looked around
On all that He had made.
He looked at His sun,
And He looked at His moon,
And He looked at His little stars;
He looked at His world
With all its living things,
And God said, *"I'm lonely still."*

Then God sat down
On the side of a hill where He could think;
By a deep, wide river He sat down;
With His head in His hands,
God thought and thought,
Till he thought, *"I'll make me a man!"*

Up from the bed of the river
God scooped the clay;
And by the bank of the river
He kneeled Him down;
And there the great God Almighty
Who lit the sun and fixed it in the sky,
Who flung the stars to the most far corner of the night,
Who rounded the earth in the middle of His hand;
This Great God,
Like a mammy bending over her baby,
Kneeled down in the dust
Toiling over a lump of clay
Till He shaped it in His own image;

Then into it He blew the breath of life,
And man became a living soul.
Amen. Amen.

("The Creation," from *The Book of American Negro Poetry*, ed.
James Weldon Johnson [New York: Harcourt, Brace, 1922])

What James Weldon Johnson has done (in language and image
that reflect his time and experience) is describe how God came
to create us in the very image of God. Johnson had the same limits that restrict any of us: the boundaries of human language in
depicting the divine, the borders of human relationships in label-
ing God's inclusiveness, the confines of human understanding in
exploring the mysteries of God. No wonder we still marvel that
God crashed through these restrictions and put on human flesh!
Christmas is about God's overcoming these very separations.

Perhaps I prefer contemporary illustration and language that
clearly include us all (using the term "human being" instead of

"man," for example), but this poignant poem by James Weldon Johnson puts the matter squarely before us: What does it mean for us to be created in the image of God? This is, after all, our story.

Try it this way: KCB, RHM, LVJ, GLJ, WBF, MME, AWG, CPM, JSB. This makes perfectly good sense to me. (Go ahead and think it; my friends have been thinking it for years!) Those initials (not in the order of this list) are ones I use as shorthand for three bishops, my college roommate, my pastor, a grandson, a classical composer, my wife, and a long-time friend. These are quick and easy ways for me to make a note about one of these persons. (Note to Bishop Edwards: I am still holding your middle name in confidence.) But there is a good chance that for you these initials are so much gibberish.

The phrase "image of God" is not unlike these initials, sounding like so much theological gibberish; it is a shorthand way of speaking of an immensely complex and transforming relationship. "Image of God" is the term God has used to reveal God's bond with us. "Image of God" is a multi-faceted jewel; what we see is dependent on which side the sun is hitting. (Or, as we shall see later, depending on which side the Son is hitting.)

Students of the Bible (and others who like to stay awake at night worrying about these things) do not agree on the meaning of the biblical phrase "image of God." Some prefer to think of "image" as representation; some see the word meaning "resemblance" or "likeness." A few folks have figured that "image" is a parallel to the ancient practice of putting depictions of the king or queen all over the region to stand in for royal power.

No matter which of these side trips give you the best view, it is apparent that humankind's being created in the image of God marks a distinctive relationship between God and humans. The doctrine of the Trinity (another subject for another day) teaches that God lives as a community of three persons, Father, Son, and Holy Spirit. If God lives in community, we who are created in God's image are also intended for community. What is the nature of that community?

The text (Genesis 1:26) admits of no exception to humanity's creation in the image of God. (Sometimes you will find people speaking of *imago dei*—ee-MAH-go DAY-ee—which is simply the classic Latin translation of "image of God.") Each of us is on equal footing in terms of God's image. That is a radical social concept. Can you not think of a few folks who seem to have been hiding behind the door when "image of God" was passed out? Such a list might range from notorious public figures to a second-cousin-twice-removed by marriage (but not removed far enough!) or the high-scoring center on a despised rival basketball team. But such a list would be faulty.

In Genesis 1:27, the point is made and then repeated (in one form of Hebrew poetry) that God has fashioned all human beings in the image: "God created humankind in his image" (that's once); "in the image of God he created them" (that's twice). Then, for good measure, the poet-writer adds, "Male and female he created them." That's three times in one short verse: all of humanity is formed in the image of God.

So, the first point is that the community for which we are created is inclusive, even of Aunt Ellen's second cousin who ended up in jail on various nefarious charges. (Please excuse me, but I have always wanted to write "various nefarious" as back-to-back words.)

The scripture reveals three characteristics of this inclusive community, three handles for picking up the nature of the relationships in this community: (a) a relationship with God, (b) a relationship with one another, and (c) a relationship with the created order.

What about our relationship with God? As the Scriptures unfold the story of creation, God makes impersonal pronouncements ("Let there be . . ."), but when it comes to the creation of human beings, God shifts into a more personal mode: "Let us make humankind . . ." It is the difference between hearing someone say, "People love people" and hearing that person say to you, "I love you." Christmas kicks it up a notch: "For God so loved the world that he gave his only Son" (John 3:16a). It's like first getting a Christmas card from a loved one and then having that person show up to give you a hug in person. Christmas is about God's showing up in person—as one of us, as a human being—in order to keep alive a relationship with us. Created in the image of God, we are intended for communion with God.

What about our relationship with one another? Genesis 2:18 puts a lens on God's intent for human connection: not good to be alone—needs helper—needs partner. In other words, each of us is incomplete without the other. To paraphrase John Donne (1572–1631): "No one is an island, entire of itself; every one is a piece of the continent" ("Devotions Upon Emergent Occasions," Meditation XVII). As a friend of mine says when she is faced with a sudden new truth: "Merciful goose grease!" This interrelatedness of humankind is soundly countercultural. Our twenty-first-century values honor individualism. How often do I walk around with an MP3 player or a cell phone closing out all worlds but the one I choose, all worlds but my own? Just how many kinds of cereals must be offered at the supermarket so I can find "mine," and how many variations of coffee must be available for me to feel I have been respected? Merciful goose grease! Is it possibly true that it is *not* all about me? Created in the image of God, we are intended for communion with one another.

What about our relationship with the created order? Not only is all the created order the context for God's creation of humankind, but God spells out how we are to relate to these flowers and radishes and deer and two-toed sloths and duck-billed platypi (or, if you prefer, platypuses). We are created in the image of God, so we are to relate to these creatures as God relates to us. We are given a kind of sovereignty (being in charge) in relation to the nonhuman creation, but it is what Robert Davidson calls "delegated sovereignty," so we stand in a responsibility to God in the exercise of that sovereignty (*The Cambridge Bible Commentary on the New English Bible*). God's call to us is not to exploit the creation but to care for it. "Dominion"—Genesis 1:26, 28—identifies the *domain* in which we have accountability. God tells the humans to subdue the earth (Genesis 1:28), but when I checked my dictionary, I found out that "subdue" does not always mean "to subjugate, to step on, to defeat." The word can also mean "to bring to cultivation." In a sense, the invitation of God to us is to help the creation become the best it can be. Created in the image of God, we are intended for communion with the created order.

But folks, we have got to reboot the computer! We have had this splendid message of our being created in God's image, but now we are getting an error message! Something has gone wrong, badly wrong. When we look in the mirror, when we look around us, when we test the environment, when we enter the privacy of our personal relationship with God, we see an image blurred, an image shattered, an image tattered. Choose your way of saying it. You and I are created in the image of God and right now that image is not looking very healthy.

Now is when we wish the story were about Adam and Eve "back then" and not about you and me right now. The Bible does not allow us the luxury of putting it all on Adam and Eve, because "Adam and Eve are we." What happened? Sin.

God wants our love of God to be freely given—not the work of some kind of spiritual automaton—so God has given us free will. And when we (Adam and Eve) were given that choice, we chose to separate ourselves from God's will, from God's intent. The narrative is familiar: we eat of the one tree that God has told us to avoid (Genesis 2:16-17; 3:3). I have always thought that if the tree had been filled with unripe persimmons, I should have had no trouble staying away from it, but I suppose that is just another way I have of trying to blame God for this mess. It is not God's choice; it is mine. It is yours. And we have chosen badly. Sin.

This is the darkness that precedes Christmas stars. This is the silence that comes before Christmas angel voices. This is the separation that happens before the invitation to come to Bethlehem.

It is half-time and we are losing. The story of Adam—what some writers call "the first Adam"—appears to be a lost cause. The toggle on each dimension of the image has been switched to off. A relationship with God? Hardly. Adam and Eve hide from God (Genesis 3:8). Love of God is replaced by fear of God

(Genesis 3:10). A relationship with each other? Hardly. The first thing Adam and Eve do after eating the forbidden fruit is try to hide their nakedness from each other (Genesis 3:7). Once the relationship with God is broken, so is the human relationship. Shame replaces freedom (Genesis 2:25; 3:7). A relationship with the created order? Hardly. Humankind is no longer at peace with creation (Genesis 3:15, 17-18). We even are thrown out of the garden where bounty and beauty shaped our days (Genesis 3:24).

Looking at us, we have to say that the image of God is, at best, fuzzy.

If that is the story of the first Adam, Christmas raises the curtain on the second Adam.

Imagine that you have not heard the traditional stories of Christmas: shepherds, manger, Bethlehem, gold, frankincense, myrrh, overcrowded inn, baby, Mary, Joseph. Instead, out of curiosity you have gone with a friend to the home of Nympha. Her house is near the farming village of Colossae in what we now call Turkey. In the distance, you can see the giant Mount Cadmus, almost nine thousand feet high. Many in the town make their living selling wool, so it is not hard to find a wrap that gives some relief from the chilly mountain air.

Although you have never met with a group of Christian believers, you are willing to give them equal time along with all the other gods you and your neighbors worship: Zeus, Artemis, Selene, and the moon god, Men. Your friend hurries you along the dusty street. "Tonight, we are going to hear a letter from Paul!" he whispers with excitement. "The letter is being passed around all the homes where our people meet. It is our turn tonight to hear it. No wonder Nympha told us all to be there by dark."

You enter the large common room of the house and are greeted warmly. After a prayer, one of the men—you do not know his name—begins to read the letter from Paul. You are not really sure who he is either. It starts out as most letters do—greetings to those who will hear it and a few words of salutation from friends who live elsewhere.

The letter gets a little more interesting when Paul starts writing about this Jesus Christ whom this crowd worships. Then you hear the words that become for you the Christmas story. Not an angel in sight. No mention of stars. No manger. Just this: "He is the image of the invisible God" (Colossians 1:15). That is the truth of Christmas with all of the greeting card illustrations left out. Merry Christmas!

If the first Adam (you and me) blurred the image of God, Jesus Christ, the second Adam, has restored that full image. When we are in communion with Jesus Christ, we are again in communion with the image of God. The image that we have broken with our sin is made whole again in Jesus Christ. It is a rather scandalous notion: that God whom we tried to trump with the cards of our own will has chosen to reveal God's very self in human form. The birth of Jesus, Christmas, is the coming of the image of God in flesh.

No wonder that Jesus Christ is the perfect image of God. "All things have been created through him" (Colossians 1:16c) and "He himself is before all things" (Colossians 1:17a) and it is in him that there is order, "all things hold together" (Colossians 1:17b).

The image is restored. The relationship with God the Father is restored, because Jesus Christ shares in the godhead. The relationship with others is restored, because Jesus Christ shares our humanity. The relationship with the created order is restored, because in Jesus Christ himself has creation occurred.

And the good news of Christmas is that we have access to this perfect image of God because God came to Bethlehem to live among us and to invite us to let our Sin be covered by the presence of God's full image, Jesus Christ, our Lord.

Just John and Jane and Jesus. It's hard to beat that as a Christmas gift!

A Time with Young Disciples

If your congregation is using purple as the seasonal color for Advent, tell the children (and adults who eavesdrop on the "children's message") that there is a reason that many churches use purple paraments (the cloths hanging from the pulpit, the lectern, the Table) during Advent. It is not just because purple is a pretty color. You might ask, "What two colors do you mix to get purple?" (Red and blue.) But a long time ago, that is not the way folks got purple. Purple came from a dye, a chemical that made things purple. The only place to get that dye was from a certain kind of snail. If someone wanted purple cloth, he or she had to get some of that dye that would turn the cloth purple. Because that dye came from snails—and it took a lot of snails to get enough dye to color a piece of cloth—it was very, very expensive to buy something that was purple. The Bible tells about a woman named Lydia who made her living doing nothing but selling purple cloth (Acts 16:14). The purple cloth was so expensive that only very rich people could buy it, so people began to think of purple as a color that only a king or queen could afford. People began to think of purple as the color of royalty.

So, when the church began to talk about Jesus as the King of kings—the best King of all—it is not surprising that churches began to use purple as the color for the Advent season, those days when we get ready to celebrate the birth of King Jesus.

If your congregation uses blue as the color for Advent, you might tell the children that the use of blue for the color of Advent was made popular by Christians in Sweden. December is a very dark month in Sweden, with daylight sometimes lasting only five or six hours each day. Do you suppose children have to go to bed when the sun goes down at 3:00 in the afternoon? Because it is so dark in Sweden during the season of Advent, Christians began to use blue in their churches. Blue was seen as a color of hope and expectation that before long there would be light. That is exactly what the Advent season promised! Jesus, the Light of the world, was about to be born. Jesus would bring light to the world! In the dark it is hard to see, and Jesus would bring light so we could see what was right to do. In the dark, it is hard to know who is standing next to you, so Jesus would bring light so we could know that he is always near us. In the dark, it is hard to know how to walk without bumping into something, so Jesus will come and bring light so we can see how to avoid things that can harm us. No wonder the Church of Sweden liked to use blue during Advent, the time when Christians look forward to the coming of Christ, the Light.

Not only that, but when artists began to paint pictures of the baby Jesus and his mother, Mary, many of them used blue as the color of the clothes that Mary wore. Why would they do that? It was not just because they liked the color blue. These artists knew that many folks thought the color blue represented "truth." (Have you ever heard anyone say that a friend is "true blue"?)

Blue—a color of hope and a color of truth. That seems to be a good reason to use blue during Advent as we get ready to celebrate the coming of Jesus, the source of our hope and who even called himself "the Truth"!

Hymns

If your congregation resists singing unfamiliar hymns (alas), consider using the text of a hymn as a responsive reading, perhaps with the choir singing a portion and the congregation responding in unison speaking. For example, use "I Want to Walk as a Child of the Light" (hymn 206 in *The United Methodist Hymnal*, 1989) with the choir starting off singing the first stanza, the congregation speaking the second, and so on. Or have a solo voice read line one, the congregation read line two, the choir read the rest of the words down to the refrain; either the choir or the congregation could sing the refrain.

Advent Wreath

Ask someone from the congregation who is usually less visible to light the first candle on the Advent wreath.

One voice: Light begins to come.
All voices: The glimmer begins.
One voice: God brings God's image into the world.
All Voices: In us? In us!
One voice: And in the Light of the world.
All Voices: Come, Lord Jesus.

Sing stanza 1 of "Light the Advent Candle" (hymn 2090 in *The Faith We Sing*).

15

Have You Thought of Doing This?

Get a baby doll and introduce the doll to the congregation as Baby Jesus. Ask someone to take the doll to a shut-in, so Baby Jesus can visit him or her during Advent. After a few days, arrange for the doll to be taken to another home, perhaps one where a new child is expected. Arrange for the doll to move from place to place, home to home, setting to setting, office to office during the Advent season. (Each person can decide how to pass on the doll.) With the doll, send a small notebook so each person can record what it meant to have Jesus as a guest during this season. On Christmas Eve, plan for the Baby Jesus doll to be a part of the Christmas Eve service. You might even read some of the comments people wrote as Jesus visited them. Some persons may make clothes for the baby; some will add a blanket or find some other way to welcome the Lord Jesus. One congregation that was predominantly Caucasian used a Black baby doll for this experience. Doing so added a poignancy and universality to the Advent story.

JESUS: THE UNLIKELY GIFT FROM GOD

Question: If you were God, how would you make your message clear? *A Thought:* Jesus was not exactly what was expected as a Messiah, but was who God wanted to give.

Scripture: Isaiah 55:1-9
Ho, everyone who thirsts,
    come to the waters;
and you that have no money,
    come, buy and eat!
Come, buy wine and milk
    without money and without price.
Why do you spend your money for that which is not bread,
    and your labor for that which does not satisfy?
Listen carefully to me, and eat what is good,
    and delight yourselves in rich food.
Incline your ear, and come to me;
    listen, so that you may live.
I will make with you an everlasting covenant,
    my steadfast, sure love for David.
See, I made him a witness to the peoples,
    a leader and commander for the peoples.
See, you shall call nations that you do not know,
    and nations that do not know you shall run to you,
because of the LORD your God, the Holy One of Israel,
    for he has glorified you.

Seek the LORD while he may be found,
   call upon him while he is near;
let the wicked forsake their way,
   and the unrighteous their thoughts;
let them return to the LORD, that he may have mercy on them,
   and to our God, for he will abundantly pardon.
For my thoughts are not your thoughts,
   nor are your ways my ways, says the LORD.
For as the heavens are higher than the earth,
   so are my ways higher than your ways
   and my thoughts than your thoughts.

Call to Worship

One Voice: Come this day to meet the unexpected.
All Voices: But we have been here before!
One Voice: But God says that God's thoughts are not like our thoughts.
All Voices: So God is the God of the unexpected!
One Voice: To a waiting people God has sent a Savior.
All Voices: Not the expected, but what was needed.
One Voice: God sent Jesus.
All Voices: And sends Jesus again.
One Voice: Born to set the people free!
All Voices: Amen! Amen! Amen!

Pastoral Prayer   12/6/20

   Almighty God, Creator of the universe, King of kings, Lord of lords, Almighty God, Designer of space and Producer of the earth, Almighty God, Judge of all humankind and Redeemer seeking to save us from ourselves, how dare we come to you in prayer! We do not think as you think; our ways are not your ways; and you hold sway over all that we claim as our own.
   Yet you loved us enough to come and live among us. You loved us enough to call us back to lives of peace and justice. You loved us enough to come and think your thoughts even in our midst, to live your truth even in the midst of our untruth, and to live a cross-shaped love that sought to save us.

18

Your grace is sufficient to speak for us in sighs that are too deep for our human language. Your grace is sufficient even when we do not recognize you because you do not look like what we expected. Your grace is sufficient even now to hear these prayers of our hearts:

(Here the one leading the prayer may include confessions, petitions, intercessions, and thanksgivings appropriate to the community.)

Hear the prayer we offer in the name of the unexpected One, even Jesus Christ our Lord, who taught us to pray, "Our Father . . ."

Some Ingredients to Stir into the Sermon Pot

Waiting for the Other Shoe to Fall

Walk with me into a grocery store. Take one of those grocery carts. They are probably a little stuck together—they always seem to be—so it will take a tug to get one separated. Ready?

We shall buy some vegetables (although maybe not any artichokes; the ones we bought last time are still in the refrigerator). Next, add kumquats and apricots to the cart, and drop in a box of cereal (two boxes for the price of one this week, so get two). Then we'll go over to the meat counter (having ignored the display of tofu) and tell the butcher we want a dollar's worth of ground beef. (The butcher will say, "Do you want me to wrap it, or did you bring your own thimble?")

So, let's fill up the cart and work our way over to the checkout. I don't know about you, but I've been adding it up in my head—about what is it going to cost (usually about ten dollars more than I had planned to spend). We wait in the line, trying to glance at the cover of a magazine we would not want our friends to see us reading. Finally, it is our turn at the checkout, so we grit our teeth and wait.

And the cashier says, "There is no charge."

"Oh, is something on special?"

"No, there is no charge for any of this: the cereal, the beef, the cucumbers. There is no charge. Your groceries are free."

The whole scene is ridiculous. No one gives away food at the grocery store. No one gives away all these things of value. But there it is: a ridiculous offer, right in the Bible.

You have to admit: this text (Isaiah 55:1-9) does not seem entirely honest. The invitation to "come, buy . . . without money" (Isaiah 55:1) sounds just a little shady. The Old Testament word that is translated *buy* is *shâbar*, a term that literally means *to deal in grain*. I get this image of a sinister sort slipping fingers onto the scales so the purchaser thinks there is more grain in the bucket than there actually is. The whole thing seems wrong. But this is what God has invited us to do: buy without money. God has offered to give away the groceries! That is potent good news!

When this passage of Isaiah (in what is sometimes called Second Isaiah because chapters 40–66 seem to have been written at a different time and by a different author than chapters 1–39) brought this revelation to the people of Israel, many of the Hebrew leaders were in exile. Some of the generation hearing these verses would have grown up in Babylon. They would never have known firsthand the joys of being in Jerusalem. They would never have known firsthand what it meant to be a free people. They would never have known what it meant to live the life of the "promised land."

When the prophet says "Come" (three times in Isaiah 55:1), he is using a term that in Hebrew is as much an exclamation as it is an invitation. Often it is used to denote grief or mourning. Maybe that is what this exiled community is feeling: grief and mourning. And then comes this offer from God: buy and eat even though you have no money.

When I hear an offer that sounds too good to be true, I wait for the other shoe to fall. And this offer from God sounds too good to be true. Can you say "unexpected"? Can you say "my thoughts are not your thoughts" (Isaiah 55:8)?

The prophet asks the question: why do you waste your time on false solutions? Why do you look into every passing whim

(Isaiah 55:2)? It is like "Why buy plastic toy food when you can have the real thing for free?"

The theological term for this free, undeserved gift is "grace." God is offering us grace. It is a radical notion. It is a countercultural concept. Grace. If I want God in my life, I can have that presence with the gift marked "Paid."

How about the prodigal son? He came back home with the bill marked "Paid."

How about the thief dying on the cross next to Jesus? He heard the Master say, "Today, you will be with me in Paradise." The bill is marked "Paid"!

How about John Wesley's finally having a gift of assurance after years of struggling to be right with God? At the meeting on Aldersgate Street, he felt his heart "strangely warmed" and said he felt that Christ's love was for him. The bill is marked "Paid"!

God's presence with us is free. But there is a problem. Sometimes you can't give it away!

Waiting for the other shoe to fall. The prodigal son's brother waited for the other shoe to fall. Surely the waiting father was not going to give this huge party for a wayward child.

Waiting for the other shoe to fall. The other thief on the cross waited for the other shoe to fall. That thief was convinced that if Jesus were for real he would get them all delivered from their crosses.

Waiting for the other shoe to fall. Those who put the limits of election on God's grace waited for the other shoe to fall. Surely, they argued, this experience of John Wesley's would not hold up under the test of time.

God is in the giving-away business, but sometimes you can't give it away. In some sense, the Advent season is needed in order to prepare us for Christmas because the gift of Christmas is so unexpected that we otherwise might miss it. Our spiritual antennae are not likely to be tuned toward a stable in Bethlehem unless a prophet looks ahead, an angel alerts, and a star invites.

We routinely comment that Jesus was not the Messiah who was expected. We note that he was a suffering servant, not a conquering military hero. We recall how he was human, not regarding "equality with God as something to be exploited" (Philippians 2:6). The surprise for the twenty-first century may be not so much the nature and character of Jesus as it is that God provides this saving presence as a gift. We don't do gift-receiving well. (If you are at a Christmas party, do you want to open a gift as everyone watches or do you prefer to watch someone else open a gift you have brought?) The unexpected plan of God is to offer this water without price (Isaiah 55:1).

Chrysostom, a bishop who lived at the turn between the fourth and fifth centuries, understood just how remarkable this gift was. He wrote:

> For if God had made us in order to punish us, we might well have despaired and questioned the possibility of our own salvation. But he created us for no other reason than his own good will, and with a view to our enjoying everlasting blessings, and if he does and contrives everything for this end, from the first day to the present time, what is there which can ever cause us to doubt? ("Letter to the Fallen Theodore," in *Ancient Christian Commentary on Scripture*, Old Testament, Vol. XI, ed. Mark W. Elliott [Downer's Grove, Illinois: InterVarsity Press, 2007])

There is an interesting thing about a word in Isaiah 55:3. God's invitation is to come to God, to listen to God, in order that we may *live*. The Hebrew word *ehelyiih* can indeed be translated *live*. But it can also be rendered *revive* or *restore*. Maybe the text could read: "Come to God that you might be revived, in order that you might be restored"—dare we say—"in order that you might be converted, transformed."

That is Advent darkness turned into Christmas light. That is Advent expectancy turned into Christmas reality. That is Advent hope turned into Christmas surprise. And that is what is available for free. Well, free to us.

So, then, why does God have trouble giving it away? Why isn't everyone thrilled to have God in her or his life? What doesn't everyone accept God's offer to be in heart and head?

I think I can tell you by sharing a story I first heard more than thirty years ago. (Please understand—I first heard this as I rested in my cradle.) It is still true.

One day a fellow was walking down the street and he came upon several boys and girls sitting on the curb, some in tears, some looking very sad, all apparently washed out. "What's the matter?" the man asked. "Did you lose the ball game?"

"No."

"Did you have a big test at school today?"

"No."

"Did one of you get mad at another?"

"No."

"Well," the man continued, "what happened?" (Pardon me while I reach for a tissue.)

One little boy said, "We've all got a pain in Jimmy's stomach." That's what happens! You let God into your life and

> we share each other's woes,
> our mutual burdens bear;
> and often for each other flows
> the sympathizing tear.
> —John Fawcett, "Blest Be the Tie That Binds," 1782

You let God into your life and you let Jimmy's stomach into your life! You let God into your life and you let the hurts of the world into your life! You let God into your life and you have taken on the children who are abused, the elderly who are forgotten, the sick who are hurting, the poor who are hungry, the lazy who are not worth it, the successful who seem not to need it, the powerful who seem not to want it.

You let God into your life and you'll never live alone again. God's presence in your life, seen most fully in Jesus Christ, is a gift to you, even if it is an unexpected gift. But when God comes into your life, God brings in all those other people whom God loves.

And because of that, the rich young ruler turned and "went away sorrowful" (Matthew 19:22 KJV). And what about us?

You can turn it down. You can turn and go away sorrowful. Maybe Advent can be seen as a time of getting ready to make that decision: stay or go. Maybe Advent can be seen as a time of getting ready to make that decision: how will we treat that baby born in Bethlehem?

God's presence is free but you can make like you do not see it. God's presence is free, but we can choose to say "no." But there is good news for those of us who do want the fullness of God's love. It's ready now and I don't have to wait to deserve it to claim it. "Without money, come and buy." Without a perfect record of good works, come and live a new life. Without having always gotten it right, come and return to the homeland.

God doesn't let go that easily! God is a seeking God, moving to set God's people free. This text is Isaiah's vision and image of how God would restore Judah from captivity in Babylon. God has not let go of Judah while that nation was in exile. And now in God's time, God is ready to restore them to their home.

God is ready to restore us to our home, to our potential, to our fullness. God still comes to our places of exile, wherever, in whatever way Jimmy's stomach hurts. It doesn't make sense, but God wants to do it without charge.

This text from Isaiah is one that shows up in the lectionary for use during Lent. That is not surprising, because the passage also includes an invitation to repent (Isaiah 55:7) because God "will abundantly pardon." It is part of God's plan. In fact, in Isaiah 55:8-9, the word interpreted as thoughts ("my thoughts are not your thoughts") is sometimes brought into English as plans. In other words (guess what!) God has plans that we would have never had on our own!

It is God's plan that Advent be turned into Christmas, that defeat be turned into victory, that exile be turned into home, that doubt be turned into love, that you and I be turned into the persons we were created to be.

A Time with Young Disciples

Ask the children if they like good surprises. (Keep in mind that there might be some children who have been abused and been told not to tell anyone. There is a difference between a secret and a surprise.) "What is the best surprise you ever had?" Give each child a small gift (a piece of candy, a toy car, a book, a piece of broccoli—well, maybe not the broccoli). Ask, "What did you do to earn this surprise?" Unless you have an unusually precocious child who wants to play "top the preacher," the children will probably reply, "Nothing."

"What do you do now that you have the surprise?" A few, no doubt products of your excellent program of Christian education, will say, "We should say 'thank you.'"

"How do you say 'thank you'?" "By saying it." "By doing good things."

On this second Sunday of Advent, we are waiting for another gift that we do not deserve: the birth of Jesus. Of course, we know that Jesus has already been born, so what is the surprise? The surprise is that Jesus can be born in each of our lives. We say "Thank you" in our words and in our deeds.

Hymns

Along with the hymns for the Advent season, explore the hymnal for other selections that bring this text from Isaiah to us musically. For example, consider singing "Come, All of You" (hymn 350 in *The United Methodist Hymnal*). If you think singing this hymn might be a bit arduous for your congregation, have four persons read the text aloud, each one reading just one stanza. The words of the hymn are drawn almost directly from Isaiah 55:1-2. If you do not have access to *The United Methodist Hymnal* or another hymnal containing this hymn, you could ask someone (who has practiced) to read one or two stanzas of the hymn. Here are stanzas 1 and 4:

> Come, all of you, come, men and women, come forward,
> drink of the water provided for you;
> all of you who are thirsty, come to me to drink
> from the water of life, provided by Jesus your Lord.
>
> Come, all of you, come, hungry and poor, come forward,
> buy your milk and wine without money;

come for free, bring no penny; come to me,
receive the bread and the water of life,
provided by Jesus your Lord.

The hymn text is from Laos and the music is from Thailand. What wonderful cues that God's grace is universal!

Hymn 124 in *The United Methodist Hymnal*, "Seek the Lord," builds on the imagery of Isaiah 55:6-11. Do you know this tune: GENEVA? Perhaps the congregation might learn it. If not, before you decide not to use this hymn text, look on pages 928 and 929 of *The United Methodist Hymnal* (or the metrical index in other hymnals). Find the heading 87.87.D. All of the tunes listed there (there are seventeen) will fit these words. Try a few of them in the privacy of your shower and choose one with which the congregation is comfortable. (All those funny numbers—87.87.D, for example—have to do with how many syllables there are in the poetry of each hymn.)

Advent Wreath

Invite a child to light the first two candles on the Advent wreath.

One voice: We light a candle to remember that Jesus is the perfect image of God.
All voices: Praise be to you, O Christ!
One voice: We light a candle to wait for God's Light to surprise us.
All voices: Praise be to you, O Christ!
One voice: Waiting itself can be a gift from God.
All voices: In God's own time, come, Lord Jesus.
One voice: Come, Lord Jesus.
All voices: Come, Lord Jesus.

Have You Thought of Doing This?

Sometime during the Advent season, sponsor a baby shower for Jesus. Perhaps following (or preceding) a service of worship, the congregation can gather in a room decorated with the usual festive baby shower arrangements. (If you want to chase a theological rabbit, ask the planning team if, because we know the gender of the baby, it is appropriate to use both pink and blue decorations? Was the fact that Jesus was male intrinsic for his salvific work? Does the fact that our Lord's gift was a universal atonement—in Christ, there is neither male nor female, Galatians 3:28—make his gender irrelevant? Does it lessen the presence of God in the real person Jesus if we do not acknowledge that person's maleness? Mercy. You may not want to mention this to the planning team.)

Let the party proceed! Have a representative (of a local homeless shelter or a home for abused women and their children or a shelter for teens with undesired pregnancies) say a word or two about that ministry. Then he or she can unwrap the gifts that have been brought. It is entirely proper to say things like "Isn't that cute?" or "Ooh, aah" or "Was I ever that small?"

The gifts, of course, are for the ministry that is in place for children. (Homeless shelters often report that diapers and baby clothes are in major demand.) Someone from the congregation could be invited to remind the assembled party that the "baby shower" really is a gift to Jesus.

It is up to you to decide how elaborate to make the invitations (just an announcement in the bulletin, a few posters?), how special to make the refreshment (punch, cookies, and, come to think of it, I don't think I've ever seen eastern North Carolina barbecue at a baby shower), and how to help your guests load up the goodies for transport to the ministry. (Children might enjoy doing this.) The baby shower would be a good occasion for a children's choir to sing. And I think there might be a special warmth in recognizing the oldest person (willing to admit it!) who is present. The love of Jesus knows no boundary of age.

JESUS: THE UNLIKELY STORY OF GOD WITH US

Question: Why isn't God a bit neater in doing the work of God?
A Thought: God is God and I am not.

Scripture: Matthew 1:18-25
 Now the birth of Jesus the Messiah took place in this way. When his mother Mary had been engaged to Joseph, but before they lived together, she was found to be with child from the Holy Spirit. Her husband Joseph, being a righteous man and unwilling to expose her to public disgrace, planned to dismiss her quietly. But just when he had resolved to do this, an angel of the Lord appeared to him in a dream and said, "Joseph, son of David, do not be afraid to take Mary as your wife, for the child conceived in her is from the Holy Spirit. She will bear a son, and you are to name him Jesus, for he will save his people from their sins." All this took place to fulfill what had been spoken by the Lord through the prophet:
 "Look, the virgin shall conceive and bear a son,
  and they shall name him Emmanuel,"
which means, "God is with us." When Joseph awoke from sleep, he did as the angel of the Lord commanded him; he took her as his wife, but had no marital relations with her until she had borne a son; and he named him Jesus.

Call to Worship
One voice: Grace and peace to you in the name of our Lord Jesus Christ.
All voices: And also with you.

One voice: We greet one another because we wait together,
All voices: As Mary and Joseph waited together.
One voice: We wait with our own struggles and doubts and wonder.
All voices: Waiting to remember. Waiting to celebrate.
One voice: To remember, to celebrate Emmanuel!
All voices: God with us!
One voice: Born to set the people free.
All voices: Amen! Amen! Amen!

Pastoral Prayer   12/13/20

"O come, O come, Emmanuel, and ransom captive Israel."
Holy God, we come again within the canopy of your great love:
your sheltering presence, your challenging purpose, your surprising grace. This day as we ponder the stumbles and strengths of Mary and Joseph, we bring to you our own confessions of Why me? our own good intentions that miss the mark, our own cautious waiting to see what you will do.

The days around us often reflect our own harried spirits. And it is into such a world you come. The flow of life around us rushes us to buy, not to honor your gift in Christ Jesus, but as if our value depends on how much we give. For some of us, we long for days that fill up with activity and joy, because these days have become times of pain and loneliness and separation. All of this we open before you, asking for the peace that the world cannot give.

You have come among us, O God. You are already Emmanuel. Our Advent wait is both to remember what it is to wait and to wait with longing for you to come again. With the willingness of Joseph and with the accepting spirit of Mary, we wait. Come, Lord Jesus.

(*Here the one leading the prayer may include confessions, petitions, intercessions, and thanksgivings appropriate to the community.*)

Hear the prayer we offer in the name of the coming peace, even Jesus Christ, our Lord, who taught us to pray: "Our Father . . ."

Some Ingredients to Stir into the Sermon Pot

An Embarrassment Named Emmanuel

As we get into this Third Sunday of Advent, in the countdown days before Christmas, most of our focus is toward the coming days: how much shopping is left to be done, plans for trips to visit family, special services to get worked out, and wondering if it is too late to return that sweater I bought my cousin (I need to return it because I saw her wearing exactly the same sweater yesterday).

Matthew must not have gotten the memo. Right in the middle of our looking ahead toward Christmas, the gospel writer begins his account of Christmas by looking back. For seventeen verses, Matthew lists name after name after name (after name, after name) of those who preceded Jesus in the line of David. Forty-two generations. That's a lot of looking back.

It's an interesting list. It includes great saints among the ancestral faithful: Abraham, Jacob, Ruth, Josiah, David, Solomon. Of course, this crew was not without its flaws, but they stand positively robust compared to the likes of Manasseh, about fifty years of ruling as king, replete with the promotion of idolatry and the worship of Baals. Then there is Rahab, prostitute extraordinaire. Of course, how about Abiud, who is famous for being the least famous of anybody in the fourteen-generation list!

Obviously, this list is made of folks "back then," who are an awful lot like folks "here and now." Maybe Matthew is trying to encourage his readers, because almost everybody can find somebody in that list who is "just like me." And these people "just like me" are the ones God used to bring the generations from Abraham to David, from David to the exile in Babylon, from the exile in Babylon to the Messiah. The list sort of evaporates my excuse that "God cannot use folks like me." God's been there and God's done that! (It remains to be seen if God also has the T-shirt.)

So, the text for this look-ahead Sunday of Advent has the preface of a text that looks back, way back.

One reason Matthew did this genealogical inventory is that he was writing primarily for readers who had Jewish background. To trace the Messiah through the spiritual inheritance of the Hebrew people was important to those of Jewish background and belief. Twenty-five times Matthew quotes scripture from what we call the Old Testament. Matthew tries to help his Jewish audience appreciate the solid Hebrew roots of the Messiah and the grounding of the life and ministry of Jesus in the history of Israel.

But notice what comes immediately after Matthew's account of the birth of Jesus. It is the story of the wise men who came to worship the Christ Child (Matthew 2:1-12). Do you see the sandwich Matthew has made? The Matthean story of the birth of Jesus is placed square dab between seventeen verses telling of his Hebrew heritage and twelve verses telling of the Gentiles who came to worship him. This Jesus is for all people: Jew and Gentile. This Jesus is a Messiah for all.

Students of the Bible do not agree about when Matthew was written. The range of estimates is from about 60 to 80 CE. On the other hand, scholars think the Letter to the Galatians was drafted approximately 40 to 50 CE. So Galatians came first. It is in Galatians 3:28 that the writer says, "There is no longer Jew or Greek, there is no longer slave or free, there is no longer male and female; for all of you are one in Christ Jesus." Now, here in this gospel account for Jewish Christians, Matthew is finding a way to say the same thing: this Jesus reaches out from his manger to hold hands both with Jew and with Gentile.

It takes Matthew only eight verses to tell about the most important birth in human history. The first time Mary appears on the scene she is already being identified as the mother of Jesus (Matthew 1:18). Without that identity as the mother of the Savior, Mary would probably have slipped into obscurity. How old was Mary when she became engaged to Joseph? Writers guess that she was between twelve and fifteen, the usual age when Jewish girls were betrothed. This betrothal (or engagement) was a notch more serious than our American cultural understanding of such a relationship. For Mary and Joseph, it was as if they had entered into a binding contract. The marriage usually came a year or so later, but "the deal was done." The couple was considered husband and wife, even if they did not move in together for a year.

Notice how many ways Matthew has of telling us that God is in the midst of this birth-gift. (1) Mary is found to be with child from the Holy Spirit. (2) An angel of the Lord appeared to Joseph in a dream. (3) The child is to be named Jesus, which means "God saves." (4) All this fulfilled what the Lord had previously spoken by the prophet. (5) This child shall be called Emmanuel, which means "God is with us."

When we talk about the virgin birth, let us not get hung up on talking about biology; the virgin birth is theology and means that God is in the midst of this.

From time to time, developers make an all-out effort to buy St. Bartholomew's Church in New York City. The building sits on a very, very valuable bit of property in the Wall Street district of the city, Park Avenue at 51ˢᵗ Street. The congregation has been offered millions on top of millions (no doubt wrapped in millions) of dollars by those who wish to build a giant office tower there. One time when these gargantuan offers were made (and turned down), the priest said, "We want to stay here. This church building is a sign that God is in this place."

So it is that Matthew tells the story of the birth of Jesus and tells the story with signs that "God is in this place." Make no mistake: the Advent-Christmas story is God's story.

But that does not make it any less messy. Sometimes God does messy work. In this short account, we have a pregnant teenager whose marriage was not finalized, a messed-up romance, the threat of a broken contract, the possibility of public disgrace, the necessity of angels showing up to straighten out things, and an on-again/off-again/on-again engagement. Not bad for eight verses! (Remember all those messy people in the genealogy of Matthew 1:1-17.) I find encouragement in that. God does not have to be absent from my life because I have a few pieces of the puzzle missing. God does not have to be absent from my life because it looks too complicated, too complex, for divine presence. In fact—who knows—God's very presence might be in the mystery of the messy!

When Matthew is inspired to remind the reader that this child is named Jesus because "he will save his people from their sins" (that is what the word "Jesus" means), he chooses the word *sōzō*. We translate it *save*, but the range of its meaning is far beyond simple rescue. The word means to make whole, to heal, to preserve, to protect. Jesus makes his people whole. Jesus heals his people. Jesus preserves his people. Jesus protects his people. And remember: we know that Matthew includes both Jews (Matthew 1:1-18) and non-Jews (Matthew 2:1-12) among "his people." The claim that Jesus will save his people from their sins was an incredibly shocking claim, because the Jewish tradition was clear that only God could save people from sin. If Jesus can save his people from their sins, his life, ministry, death, resurrection must be the story of God's very self among us. Emmanuel! God is with us! The story of Jesus' birth is a divine story.

But it is also a human story. Jesus was Mary's son, and when Matthew tells us that (Matthew 1:21, 25), he uses the Greek word that is used for any human child. It is even more earthy than that. The same word (*huiets*) is used to tell about the foal of a mare. This is birth talk. This is not some sudden, fully grown arrival of a god. Numerous religions of the time told of their gods arriving on earth, but they came fully primed and ready. This is a baby, a human baby, a son born of a human mother. Has humanity had a higher moment than when God came among us as a human being?

Jesus came as a baby, not dropped full-blown into human history, but delivered after Mary had her full portion of morning sickness and sleepless nights worrying if her newborn would be all right, ten toes, ten fingers. God's story is a human story.

When the Apostles' Creed was being developed, the phrase "born of the Virgin Mary" was included not to emphasize *virgin* Mary, but to make the point that Jesus was *born* of the Virgin Mary. Jesus was born. The Nicene Creed says "truly human."

In these few verses, Matthew opens up the theological principle that Jesus was fully human and fully divine. The preparation days of Advent carry with them the anticipation, excitement, anxiety, and expectation of any human birth. And because the

Advent season is also about preparation and readiness for the final coming of Jesus (some call it the second coming), these four weeks renew in our time the same anticipation, excitement, anxiety, and expectation of the first coming.

This wonderful, sacred, holy story has its setting among a couple in love, a man not willing to disgrace his wife, a mother and father struggling to do the right thing. The wonderful, sacred, holy story is also a human story. God is in the human business. That is great, freeing-up good news.

When our son was in college, he commented that the students were complaining about the food in the dining hall. This grumbling is almost a rite of passage for undergraduates. The focus of the protest was the breakfast food: "The eggs are not for real," they argued. "You are using those powdered things, not fresh eggs," the students lamented.

One morning when the early-riser students (is that a contradiction in terms?) entered the dining hall for breakfast, there was on display a large silver punch bowl. It was filled with cracked, freshly emptied eggshells. Next to it was a sign: "Yes, we do so use real eggs!"

The story at Bethlehem is the story of God's giving us a sign that says, "Yes, my love is real." Jesus is God's way of saying, "Yes, we do so use real love!"

When Matthew quotes Isaiah 7:14 ("and [they] shall name him Immanuel"), he teaches us some Hebrew language. The word *Emmanuel*, Matthew explains, means *God with us*. The Hebrew word draws on two words: the word *ʾêl*—meaning *strength* or *mighty* and a name used for the Almighty God, and the word *ʿîm*—meaning *with* or *alongside*. Isaiah might not have known about whom he spoke, but Matthew surely did! In Jesus, God has come alongside us. Emmanuel!

In one place, the text says this child is to be named "Jesus" (Matthew 1:21, 25). In another place, the text says this child is to be named "Emmanuel" (Matthew 1:23). There is no conflict here. The word translated *name* (*ŏnŏma*) means *character* or *authority*. (Some students of languages think the Greek word is rooted in a word meaning *knowledge*. Thus we get knowledge of a person's character and authority by knowing the person's name.) The character and authority of Jesus is both: "he will save his people from their sins"—Jesus and "God is with us." Emmanuel.

But why might we say that Jesus is "an embarrassment named Emmanuel"? Consider the frightened Mary. Was she embarrassed to tell her family that she was pregnant even though she and Joseph had not consummated their marriage? Consider the perplexed Joseph. Was he embarrassed to have his friends go "wink, wink"—"so you and Mary have not been together, but she is pregnant?" Consider the village people of Nazareth. Would they be embarrassed that one of their own was claiming that she had a special message from the Holy Spirit? Consider the parents of Mary and Joseph. Probably they had arranged this marriage— that was the custom—and now would they be embarrassed to have this unexpected blip on the sonogram? There was enough embarrassment to go around.

This story is not an easy story, but one filled with struggle and shame. In that mix of emotions and surprises and expectations, I hear an invitation to bring my own emotions, surprises, and expectations to the God who is with us. It is as W. H. Auden wrote in his epic poem *For the Time Being: A Christmas Oratorio.* The poem is over fifty pages long and emerged from Auden's anguish during some of the most difficult days of World War II. As he described the birth of Christ, the poet wrote, "Now and forever, we are not alone."

A Time with Young Disciples

If your worship space has a Chrismon tree, this would be a good service in which to invite the children to gather around the tree. Be prepared to explain the significance of any of the monograms. (The word *Chrismon* combines the word *Christ* and the word *monogram*.) Leading questions might be: Which is your favorite Chrismon? Which one is nearest the top of the tree? Do you see one that looks like two letters—P and X? (Point out, of course, that these are the first two letters in the Greek word for Christ—*chi rho*, in the United States usually pronounced "ki row," rhyming with "high row.") Do you see one that you do not understand? Perhaps some of the men and women who made the monograms for the Chrismon tree could join you and help explore the symbols. (The first Chrismon tree was at Ascension Lutheran Church in Danville, Virginia, in 1957. The congregation's Web site, appropriately enough, is www.chrismon.org. Check out that Web site for stories, pictures, accounts, and a photograph of the most recent Chrismon tree at that church.)

If there is no Chrismon tree in your worship space, use this teaching puzzle. Prepare in advance by writing the word *God* in large letters on one side of a piece of heavy-stock paper. (You could use a 5-x-8-inch index card.) On the reverse side of the paper, paste a picture of Jesus (preferably one that shows him in the manger at Bethlehem). Cut the card into random pieces of differing shapes and sizes. When the children gather, spread out the puzzle with the sides with the word *God* on top. Ask the children to put the puzzle together. (When you cut the puzzle pieces, be sure to take into account how many children will be present and their skill level at putting puzzles together!) After the puzzle is assembled, tape the pieces together so the paper is re-assembled with the word *God* visible. Talk for a moment about the word *God* and how God is with us. Then say, "Let me show you one way we know that God is with us." Turn over the paper and show the picture of Jesus. If all goes well, you will have an assembled paper with *God* on one side of the paper and a picture of Jesus on the other. (If all does not go well, consider screaming at the children, "You little brats! You have messed up my story!" Consider that briefly, but then please decide not to say that. Instead, you could simply explain what you had been trying to do and ask the children if they know how you might fix whatever problem has occurred.) Remind the children that if we want to know what God is like, we can look at Jesus (loving, healing, caring, faithful, forgiving, expecting the best). By turning the paper back and forth, alternately showing the word *God* and the picture of Jesus, you can give emphasis to your point. If it seems suitable for the learning level of the children who are part of your group, you could introduce the word *Emmanuel* as meaning *God with us*, reading Matthew 1:21-23.

Hymns

Do you have persons in your congregations who might try to write a hymn for the congregation to sing? Unless they also have considerable creative musical gifts, they will probably want to select a tune they already know. One tune that could be used is HYFRYDOL. It is an easy tune and one that fits the Advent season because it is so often matched with Charles Wesley's Advent hymn "Come, Thou Long-Expected Jesus." (This hymn appears in many hymnals; it is 196 in *The United Methodist Hymnal*.)

To write a hymn text that matches the tune, your budding poet (maybe you?) will need to write words that have the same rhyming pattern and the same places of emphasis as the words that go with the tune being borrowed. For example, if HYFRY-DOL is the tune being used, notice how the words rhyme:

> Come, thou long-expected *Jesus*,
> born to set thy people FREE;
> from our fears and sins re*lease us*,
> let us find our rest in THEE.
> Israel's strength and conso*lation*,
> hope of all the earth thou ART;
> dear desire of every *nation*,
> joy of every longing HEART.

The simplest way for an inexperienced hymn writer to work would be to write a text that rhymes the same way.

The hymn poet using a preselected tune has to watch out for something else: is the accent emphasis in what is being written the same as in the text with the tune I am using?

Here is an example using boldface to show which syllable is accented:

> **Come,** thou **long** ex-**pect**-ed **Je**-sus,
> **born** to set thy **peo**-ple **free;**
> from our **fears** and **sins** re-**lease** us,
> **let** us **find** our **rest** in **thee.**
> **Is**-rael's **strength** and **con**-so-**la**-tion,
> **hope** of **all** the **earth** thou **art;**

dear de-**sire** of ev-ery **na**-tion,
joy of ev-ery **long**-ing **heart**.

Read those verses aloud, overemphasizing the words in bold. You will get a sense of the flow of the text. No word has an accent or emphasis that is different from the usual pronunciation of the word. (For example, we would not usually pronounce *expected* with the accent anywhere other than on the middle syllable: ex-**pect**-ed.)

Now turn your poetic instincts loose! Write an Advent hymn. What themes do you want to include? Hope? God with us? Waiting? As you work, keep in mind that most folks say there is no word that rhymes with *orange!*

Once the hymn text is completed, print or project the words and use the text in an Advent service. (In a similar vein, a confirmation class might work on a hymn to be sung on the Sunday of confirmation.) Once you start the ball rolling on the joy of composing hymns, no telling where it might lead!

Advent Wreath

Ask a family to come together to light the Advent wreath. As the reading is done, they will light, in sequence, the first three candles.

One voice: One candle. The light is small.
All voices: Shine brightly, Lord Jesus.
One voice: Another candle. The light begins to bloom.
All voices: Come quickly, Lord.
One voice: Candle three. More light is here.
All voices: God in our midst! Emmanuel!
One voice: And in the Light of the world.
All voices: Come, Lord Jesus.

Sing the first three stanzas of "Light the Advent Candle" (hymn 2090 in *The Faith We Sing*).

Have You Thought of Doing This?

Most congregations have members or constituents who are not able to be at the gathering place during the Advent season: persons with illness or mobility issues, who are a long distance from home (and, occasionally, I suppose, those who are simply mad at the preacher). What are some ways to let these persons enjoy the spiritual harvest of the Advent season?

One tradition is caroling. Usually, it is probably best to let people know you are coming. Does the person you are visiting have a favorite seasonal hymn? Can you encourage the person you are visiting to join in singing? With assistance, could he or she go with you to sing somewhere else? If someone is too far away to come home for the holiday, how about recording the caroling or making arrangements for him or her to put the cell phone on speakerphone as the home folks sing? Some persons are in settings where it would be disturbing to others to have a large group come. In those situations, how about a soloist? If local ordinances about loud music (and amateur singing!) permit, why not put on coats, load up a van, roll down the windows, and ride around populated areas, singing seasonal music?

Another way to reach out to those who cannot get to the church building is to bring them some object from the worship space. How about a Chrismon from the tree that is in the sanctuary? Or the "God/Jesus" puzzles that the children have made (see "A Time with Young Disciples")? How about a tape recording of greetings made by friends who were able to be at the Advent service? How about taking or sending a giant homemade card that the individual could sign and have sent back to the church? (For many shut-ins it would be special to have such a card made by the children of the church.) How about providing the homebound (or away from home) member with a list of prayer concerns from the congregation and invite her or him to be part of the congregation's "prayer warriors"?

Sometimes, persons who have been sick for a long time are embarrassed to be seen because "I just don't look like myself anymore." Another might not want to come to the service with a wheelchair because "I'll just be in the way." Someone else might be uncertain about getting out in public because "I never know when nature will call." Some persons hesitate to attend corporate worship because "I might catch a germ." To encourage these persons to be a part of the community's gathered life, make careful arrangements for them to have transportation, and invite them to a special service intended primarily for those who cannot usually attend. Maybe it would reassure some to know a nurse will be present. Would it support another if hand sanitizer was used by each one who came? Make certain that the worship space is arranged so wheelchairs and walkers can fit comfortably. Some core members of the congregation can be invited to attend this special service. The service itself should reflect the traditions with which the participants are most familiar. Ideally, those who are homebound would from time to time be a part of the regular services of the season, but this special service could provide the only alternative for some.

JESUS: THE UNLIKELY MESSIAH

Question: What does God in our midst look like?
A Thought: God does not always act as we expect a nice God to act.

Scripture: John 7:25-31

Now some of the people of Jerusalem were saying, "Is not this the man whom they are trying to kill? And here he is, speaking openly, but they say nothing to him! Can it be that the authorities really know that this is the Messiah? Yet we know where this man is from; but when the Messiah comes, no one will know where he is from." Then Jesus cried out as he was teaching in the temple, "You know me, and you know where I am from. I have not come on my own. But the one who sent me is true, and you do not know him. I know him, because I am from him, and he sent me." Then they tried to arrest him, but no one laid hands on him, because his hour had not yet come. Yet many in the crowd believed in him and were saying, "When the Messiah comes, will he do more signs than this man has done?"

Call to Worship

One Voice: We gather to worship God.

All Voices: We worship our Creator, who formed us in God's very image.

One Voice: We gather to be surprised by God.

All Voices: We worship God, the Wind that blows where it will.

One Voice: We gather to celebrate God with us.
All voices: We worship Emmanuel.
One Voice: We gather to get to know the Messiah.
All Voices: We worship and move toward a cross-shaped manger.
One Voice: Christ Jesus! Born to set the people free!
All Voices: Amen! Amen! Amen!

Pastoral Prayer

Eternal triune God, forever living in a relationship of love, we honor the community of grace within which you live. We praise you for the creative Word that became flesh and dwelt among us. We praise you for the freshness of your promise to come again. We praise you for the faces of this Advent season: looking back on a journey with the babe of Bethlehem, looking around at the presence of the risen Christ, looking ahead to the fulfillment of your reign on earth as it is in heaven.

During these final days of Advent, we sense that the star that shone over the Bethlehem stable is again offering its first rays of light upon our world. In that light, merciful One, we see the shadows of those who are hungry, the hiddenness of those who are homeless, the unrelenting pain of the victims of injustice, the shallowness of our arguments with others, and our all-too-readiness to depend on force to show who is right. You came among us and turned such a world upside down, scattering "the proud in the thoughts of their hearts," bringing "down the powerful from their thrones," lifting "up the lowly," filling "the hungry with good things," and sending "the rich away empty." Do we dare pray, *Lord: do it again?* Do we dare risk our own place in the world to make room for the Messiah who lives among us?

Bring the light, Holy One, not only that we might better see the needs around us and within us, but that we might see the path that leads to justice and righteousness and wholeness.

(Here the one leading the prayer may include confessions, petitions, intercessions, and praises appropriate to the community.)

42

Now show us clearly the saving Messiah, who himself taught us to pray, "Our Father . . ."

Some Ingredients to Stir into the Sermon Pot

Life in an Unexpected Lane

It was time to party. Every road leading into Jerusalem was filled with pilgrims making their way to the seven-day Feast of Tabernacles. Tents and huts sprung up all over the city as travelers tried to find room for their family and travel belongings. The festival was an autumn celebration of harvest. The temporary housing arrangements reminded the believers of the time their ancestors had lived in tents crossing the wilderness toward the promised land. Recalling how the Lord provided water for the Israelites, the visitors to Jerusalem carried water from the Pool of Siloam to the temple. The hurry-scurry of the week, renewing old ties, the excitement of the crowd—it was a kind of Mardi Gras without the beads.

Although Jesus was a popular teacher, he had gotten into Jerusalem without anyone much noticing. Some wondered where he was (John 7:11). Others argued about Jesus, some saying he was a good man and others saying he was a fraud (John 7:12). In the middle of all this hubbub about Jesus, he showed up at the temple "and began to teach" (John 7:14). What happened next was what often happened when Jesus spoke clearly (or when the Word is openly proclaimed). The crowd was divided on how to respond.

"You have a demon!" (John 7:20). Where did he get such book-learning? (John 7:15). Can it be that deep down the powers that be think he is the Messiah? (John 7:26). He can't be the Messiah because we know too much about this man! (John 7:27). In other words, should we pay attention to him or not?

Some have said that such questions may be the most important ones a person ever answers: *What shall I do about Jesus? Do I obey? Do I follow? Do I ignore? Do I trust? Do I forget? Do I waver? Do I honor?* Rest assured: your life is going to be different depending on how you answer those questions!

John 7:25-31 is not usually considered an Advent text. But why not? These verses are "wait and see" verses. These verses are "has he really come?" verses. These verses are "longing for the Savior" verses. These verses are "what's this baby going to grow up to do?" verses. These verses are "is God really among us?" verses. These are Advent verses.

There was a tradition that the Messiah would come anonymously (only to be revealed later by Elijah), so when some of the crowd recognized that they knew Jesus' home zip code, they immediately concluded that he could not be the Messiah. It was not the first time that God had broken tradition! (I'm not sure that God ever broke tradition by sitting in someone else's pew, but I suppose that is another matter.)

This out-loud wondering if the Messiah could be someone the people knew (John 7:27) moves us to explore a larger question: What will the Messiah be like? Known? Recognized? Conqueror? Healer? Servant? Victor? Victim? In these days of Advent, when we relive the waiting for the birth of the Messiah, we might well ponder these things that so stirred the first-century community.

Of course, we have the advantage of having read the end of the book. We know how the story ends. In fact, the Gospel writers (Matthew, Mark, Luke, John) also know how the story ends. After all, they are writing decades after the resurrection of our Lord.

John makes an interesting choice in quoting Jesus in John 7:28: "The one who sent me is true." In this Gospel, when he wants a word that means *true*, the writer alternates between two words. One of the words (*alēthinŏs*) means *true* or *truth*, as in *nothing is concealed*. The facts are all on the table and they all measure up. The other word is *apĕlĕgmŏs*—*refute* as in challenging a misimpression, making right a misinterpretation, turning around a mistake. Which word do you think John used when he quoted Jesus as saying "the one who sent me is *true*"?

It is the second word, the one that means *refute*. What our Lord says to the gathered crowd at the temple is that the one who sent him (the One he called Father) has to clear up a few things—to refute a few things—and one of those things was some bad guesses you have made about the Messiah.

When we move with Advent expectancy toward the manger, what do we expect to *see* when we get there? A baby? Yes. A nursing mother? Yes. A righteous Joseph? Yes. But if that is all we see, we have failed to see the looming shadow of a cross; we have failed to see the cold clamminess of a tomb; we have failed to see folded grave clothes in an empty tomb (and we might have failed to see a Savior whose power is among us now through the Holy Spirit). Messiah is all that, and "the one who sent Jesus" has to refute the notion that the story ends with a skin-soft baby; has to refute the notion that the Messiah is politically powerful, that the Messiah wins with a sword. No wonder John the Gospel writer chose to name the refuting kind of truth. John knew that those who saw Jesus as Messiah were driving in an unexpected lane.

Messiah, of course, is a Hebrew word that comes into Greek as *Christ*. (No, Sammy, "Christ" is not Jesus' last name.) The word means *the anointed one* and comes from a root term meaning *to rub with oil*. Anointing with oil was a traditional way of consecrating someone (a king, a ruler, a priest) for a special task. It is not surprising that the Hebrew people latched onto the term *Messiah* to name the one God would send to save God's people.

Have you ever had a nickname? I had a childhood friend we all called "Stinker." (I'll leave to your imagination and olfactory resources to figure out why we started calling him that.) Teenagers can be cruel with nicknames; we called (even in the senior yearbook) one of our classmates "Hunk-a-Chunk" because of the amplitude of her physical presence. I listened to a major league baseball game the other night, and the radio announcer kept referring to one star player as "The Man." We sometimes use nicknames as a shorthand way of referring to a friend (or enemy!), trying by the appellation to capture something of who he or she is. If we try to capture something of who Jesus is by calling him "Messiah" or "Christ," what are we trying to say?

It depends on what we think those words mean. John 7:30 points the way to what these words mean: "They tried to arrest him, but no one laid hands on him, *because his hour had not yet come*" (emphasis added). His ministry, his presence, his life is to be defined by that hour that had not yet come. His "who-ness" is to be made distinct by that hour that had not yet come. Why would John try to summarize all that Jesus did as if it could be contained in an hour? Why would John look ahead as if some hour still to come would capture all that the Messiah had been about? Why would John never really dwell on the scene at the manger, but instead write about something that had not yet happened?

It takes the Gospel writer John four chapters to write about that hour. He takes almost 150 verses to tell about that hour. It begins with betrayal and ends with resurrection. Jesus' ministry has given a sampler of what the reign of God will be like. And when his hour does come, when the crucifixion makes its painful, but unsuccessful, effort to defeat that reign, we have the full picture of who was in that manger in Bethlehem.

Let your imagination roam a bit. Elias had been a young shepherd about thirty years earlier. He often recalled going out to the fields with his uncle, watching sheep, enjoying the night air, and listening as his uncle and his friends exchanged stories about the wild beasts that sometimes came to attack the flock. (Elias knew his uncle well enough to know that his uncle would be the hero in any story the uncle told!) He had started going out to the fields when he was about nine, and my, how his parents did worry about "our little boy" out there in the dark with those ferocious wolves! "Uncle Eber, please take good care of him!"

And Uncle Eber did. He watched over Elias as he would have watched over his own son. Night after night. Month after month. By the time Elias was fourteen, he could handle the night duty as well as his aging uncle. And before long, Elias was spinning his own yarns—some of them, like good preacher stories, almost true—and deciding that he would just love to be a shepherd for the rest of his life.

One night, Elias, his Uncle Eber, and a couple of other shepherds were doing the night shift. For all practical purposes, they lived in the field, because that seemed to be all the life they knew. On this particular night—it was if it happened yesterday—all of a sudden, out of the clear blue, an angel showed up. There was so much light that it scared them all. Elias tried not to show his fear, but he moved his slender body just a little closer to his robust Uncle Eber.

The angel said, "Not to worry! I know this is a bit unusual, but I am bringing you some good news. Over in town, there has been a baby born." ("What's the big deal?" mumbled Uncle Eber. "Babies are born all the time.") The angel then said the most amazing thing: "This baby is the Messiah." That word drove straight into the heart of Elias. He knew that his people had long looked for the Messiah to come—and he knew that there had been some false alarms.

Elias looked to see how Uncle Eber was taking all this. The older man looked strangely nervous, ill at ease, not like his usual confident "ready to handle anything" self. The angel told them how the baby might be recognized ("The Messiah wrapped in bands of cloth?" wondered the young shepherd), and then the skies turned up the volume and tons of angels began to sing together:

> "Glory to God in the highest heaven,
>   and on earth peace among those whom he favors!"

As suddenly as the noise had interrupted the night, so now the quiet resumed with quickness and a new eeriness. The men looked at one another. They looked at the sheep. They looked at Elias. "Young man," the oldest of the shepherds said, "we've got to go check out this thing. It just might be true. But we can't leave all these sheep alone. You stay here while we go into town."

Elias, now not feeling quite so ready to be a grown-up shepherd, looked to his Uncle Eber for help, at least for advice. Eber smiled, put his hand on Elias's shoulder and said simply, "You can do it. The Lord be with you."

The rest of the story is pretty well known. The shepherds went into Bethlehem and found Mary, Joseph, and Jesus. "Wow!" whispered Eber. "This is just as the angel said. Do you suppose"—he paused—"do you suppose that this tiny baby could be the Messiah?"

The three men told everybody they saw what they had found that night in the stable in back of the inn. "When I went into that cave," Eber smiled, "I didn't know what to expect, but there he was! If the angel was right about where that baby would be, I think the angel was right about his being the Messiah!"

By the time the shepherds got back to the fields, Elias was too tired to hear the strange story they were trying to tell. But the next night, he was back in the field, and the next night, and the next. He was plainly the shepherd who got left behind to care for the sheep, always feeling left out of that special night.

Now it was thirty years later. Now Elias was in Jerusalem. Now he heard again the wondering of those around him: "Do you suppose that man could be the Messiah?" Elias, no longer a youth but now a man of late years for that time, watched and listened as Jesus spoke. Elias thought to himself, "I didn't get my chance thirty years ago. This is no baby and this is not Bethlehem and I hear no angel voices, but I must know."

So Elias, now bent from years of keeping sheep, walked over to the man some called Messiah. Elias asked, "Are you Messiah? Are you the Shepherd of our flock?" Jesus smiled.

A Time with Young Disciples

Once the children gather, start with a story. "One time there were a little boy and little girl who were brother and sister. They loved each other, but they argued a lot—do any of you argue with your brother or sister?" In advance, make arrangements to have someone call your cell phone. Be sure to have it on the loudest possible ring (and be sure to have it with you!). When the phone rings, look puzzled and answer the phone (if it doesn't ring, your puzzled look will be for real). Listen for a moment and then say to the children, "I just got the strangest call. Somebody called and said they had good news for me. What do you suppose the good news could be?" (Answers might range from "you won the lottery" to "your grandchildren are coming to visit" or "your grandchildren are going home after a visit" or "the Panthers won the game last night.")

Say to the children: "That call interrupted the story I was telling, but don't you think I should go and check out the good news?" Get up and tell the children you'll be right back. (This would be a good Sunday to have an extra adult or two with you during this time with the young disciples.) If possible, go out of the room; at least, go to a far corner. After fifteen seconds (it will seem like thirty minutes) come back in and say, "Would you like to know what the good news was?"

Even if the children mumble that they couldn't care less about your good news, plow ahead. "The good news was that I would get to see Jesus today! How do you think that could happen?" (Allow time for an answer or two.)

"Well, Jesus said that where two or three were gathered in his name, he would be there in the midst of them. We have two or three and lots more gathered here in Jesus' name, so Jesus is here in our midst!

"Jesus said that when we feed a hungry person, we are feeding Jesus. When we get clothes for someone who needs clothes, we get clothes for Jesus. Jesus said that when we are a friend to someone who needs a friend, we are a friend to Jesus. I think I am going to have a lot of chances to see Jesus today!

"It is almost Christmas, and maybe we wish we could have been in Bethlehem so we could have seen the baby Jesus. Well, that is what my good news was: we can see Jesus today when we meet in his name and when we help people in his name. The shepherds were surprised when the angel told them to go to Bethlehem to see the newborn baby. I was surprised to get a call today to go see Jesus. What a good Christmas present to get a few days early!"

By arrangement, have your colleague dial your cell phone again. Answer it and this time hold it up to the children and to the congregation and say, "It's for you."

Hymns

If someone (or more than one) has written an Advent hymn (see "Hymns" in the Third Sunday of Advent, pages 37-38), you could use one or two of them in this service.

Either in a bulletin or by announcement, tell the story behind some of the seasonal hymns you are singing.

Here is an example. (Of course, you can present a briefer account):

James Montgomery was born in 1771 in Scotland. His parents were Moravian missionaries and by the time James was twelve years old, they left him in Scotland while they went to do mission work in the West Indies. They both died while they were gone and were buried in foreign countries. James did not see them after he was twelve. Because he did not do well in school, he was allowed to leave formal learning and to pursue a career as a baker. Evidently, his buns were no better than his books, so after a year and a half he left the bakery.

Montgomery eventually went to London and tried to get some of his poems published. No luck. But he did connect with a man who edited and printed a newspaper, and eventually Montgomery was editing and printing the paper himself. He did this for thirty-two years.

James Montgomery was active in political affairs and, because of it, ended up in prison a couple of times. Once he was jailed because he made the local community look bad by reporting on a riot that broke out in the town. The other time, he was in prison for almost two years because he published a poem in which there was praise for the fall of the Bastille in the French Revolution. Although by now his religious fervor had faded, he took on causes of justice, including strongly protesting slavery when that trade was a boon for the wealthy in Britain's economy.

By the time James Montgomery was forty-three, he sought again the witness of the church. He resumed a place in the Moravian tradition and, renewing his dormant interest in writing poetry, began writing poems and hymn texts. One of the hymns he wrote was "Hail to the Lord's Anointed," a paraphrase of Psalm 72. Montgomery quoted the hymn at the end of a lecture he was giving at a Wesleyan missionary conference. It was so well received that others began to quote it and sing it.

The power of Montgomery's commitment shows up in stanza two:

> He comes with succor speedy
> to those who suffer wrong;
> to help the poor and needy,
> and bid the weak be strong

and (in stanza three) his vision of peace and righteousness. (Include here a note about where your congregation might find the hymn text; it is in many hymnals, including *The United Methodist Hymnal*, hymn 203.)

Once James Montgomery began to write hymns (at the age of forty-three), he produced more than four hundred, many of which are sung widely. For example, in addition to "Hail to the Lord's Anointed," there are "Angels from the Realms of Glory," "Go to Dark Gethsemane," "Prayer Is the Soul's Sincere Desire," and "Stand Up and Bless the Lord" (all in *The United Methodist Hymnal* and many other hymnals).

James Montgomery was eighty-three when he died. His hymns live on.

Advent Wreath

Invite someone who might be alone for the first time this Christmas to be the one who lights the four Advent candles.

One voice: Light. The image of God.
All Voices: Be light in our darkness, O Christ
One voice: Light. The pathway of Jesus.
All Voices: You are light and in you is no darkness.
One Voice: Light. God is with us.
All Voices: Already the true light is shining.
One Voice: Light. The Messiah comes!
All Voices: You are the light of the world.

One Voice: In him there is no darkness at all. The night and
             the day are both alike.
All Voices: **The night is as light as the day.**
One Voice: And in the Light is no darkness.
All Voices: **Come, Lord Jesus**

(Adapted from "Canticle of Light and Darkness, #205 *The United
Methodist Hymnal*, 1989)

Have You Thought of Doing This?

The holiday season is a difficult time for those who have lost
loved ones during the year or who have experienced a family
break-up or who live under illness's cold grip. Plan a Service of
Remembrance and Healing. This might well be offered on the
evening of the Fourth Sunday of Advent. If your congregation
has trained Stephen Ministers, this service is a good time and
place for them to offer their ministries.

Keep in mind that, for some, the worship space will be a place
filled with memories. Perhaps a funeral was in this place. Perhaps
a deceased loved one donated the funds to buy a window. Perhaps
a marriage, now dissolved, took place here. Perhaps there is the
flood of remembrance of being anywhere "we used to do things
together." It will probably be sufficient just to acknowledge this
so persons will not think, *Something is wrong with me because I am
feeling this way.*

Even though the Advent and Christmas seasons are a highly
significant and moving time in the congregation's life, some pastors already feel the burden of having to lead multiple services
during the holiday period. If this is the case with you, consider
inviting a hospital chaplain or a hospice chaplain to preach.
(Even though the pastor may not preach, those who gather do
need to see their pastor as part of the service leadership.)

The service can include singing, scripture, prayer, proclama-
tion, and gentle sharing. One theme that could be preached is
from John 1:46: "Can anything good come out of Nazareth?"
That same question stirs in many hearts when there is loss and
brokenness: *Can anything good come out of this?* Nazareth was a

paltry village and, by all appearances, would not be celebrated or enjoyed or valued in any way. But God did something in Nazareth! Because God came into Nazareth, something good indeed did come from this place that held no promise. Our losses seem to hold no promise for tomorrow. Our hurting places seem to project nothing that is good. But the God who went into Nazareth can come into our emptiness, our pain, our wound, our uncertainty. Can anything good come out of Nazareth? In Christ Jesus, the answer is "yes."

If the group is not too large, the service can close with those present gathering around the Table. From a candle representing the presence of Christ, each one can light another candle and place it on the Table. Some may wish to call aloud the name of the one they are recalling as they light the candle. Form a circle. If it seems to be a comfortable thing for all to do, invite those present to hold hands. This would be a time of support as anyone who wishes offers some memory of the one(s) he or she remembers.

After the service, Stephen Ministers or other caring persons should be available to listen to the stories and grief of those who have gathered.

In some settings, it will be appropriate to anoint persons with oil while having individual prayers with them.

JESUS: AN UNLIKELY PEACEMAKER

Question: What does great fear have to do with the birth of Jesus?
A Thought: Encountering Jesus is not always peace and light.

Scripture: Luke 2:8-20

In that region there were shepherds living in the fields, keeping watch over their flock by night. Then an angel of the Lord stood before them, and the glory of the Lord shone around them, and they were terrified. But the angel said to them, "Do not be afraid; for see—I am bringing you good news of great joy for all the people: to you is born this day in the city of David a Savior, who is the Messiah, the Lord. This will be a sign for you: you will find a child wrapped in bands of cloth and lying in a manger." And suddenly there was with the angel a multitude of the heavenly host, praising God and saying,

"Glory to God in the highest heaven,
    and on earth peace among those whom he favors!"

When the angels had left them and gone into heaven, the shepherds said to one another, "Let us go now to Bethlehem and see this thing that has taken place, which the Lord has made known to us." So they went with haste and found Mary and Joseph, and the child lying in the manger. When they saw this, they made known what had been told them about this child; and all who heard it were amazed at what the shepherds told them. But Mary treasured all these words and pondered them in her heart. The shepherds returned, glorifying and praising God for all they had heard and seen, as it had been told them.

Call to Worship
One Voice: There is good news! The Christ is born!
All Voices: There is good news! The Christ is born!
One Voice: Glory to God in the highest!
All Voices: Glory to God in the highest!
One Voice: O come, let us adore him!
All Voices: O come, let us adore him!
One Voice: Born to set the people free!
All Voices: Amen! Amen! Amen!

Pastoral Prayer
"O holy Child of Bethlehem,
descend to us, we pray;
cast out our sin, and enter in,
be born in us today.
We hear the Christmas angels
the great glad tidings tell;
O come to us, abide with us,
our Lord Emmanuel!"

[Phillips Brooks, ca. 1868]

Gracious God, how easily the words of Christmas roll off our tongues. We are warmed by their familiarity and sometimes settle for our past, rather than hearing that your gift of the Christ is as new today as it was two thousand years ago. By the power of your Spirit, love is in the present tense. By the goodness of your grace, we claim not that God *was* love but that God *is* love.

You have walked this earth, holy Jesus, so you know what it is like to live in a broken place. You have embraced lepers with peace, so you know what it is like to be among those the world rejects. You have fed those who brought only their hunger, so you know what it is like to find haves and have-nots. You have seen the beauty of lilies and heard the chirping of sparrows, so you know what it is like to care for the created order. You have borne blame for sins you did not commit, so you know what it is like to hear cries of injustice.

You have been here, Lord. You *are* here, Lord. From Bethlehem to this place is only the distance of a heart of faith, so we receive gladly the news of your birth again—and again—and again—and again.

(Here the one leading the prayer may include confessions, petitions, intercessions, and thanksgivings appropriate to the community.)

Hear the prayer we offer in joy and awe and hope, even as you have taught us to pray, saying "Our Father . . ."

Some Ingredients to Stir into the Sermon Pot

Does Jesus Scare You?

Maybe the edges have worn off the story for us. We think of the peaceful, quiet night when Jesus was born. All those cards on the mantelpiece (or in the wicker basket we have always used to save cards) seem calm. "All is calm, all is bright."

There is a different scene in Luke's account. When the shepherds see the messenger angel, they are flat scared. The New Revised Standard Version says "they were terrified." The Contemporary English Version says "they were frightened." The New English Bible says "they were terror-stricken." Today's English Version says "they were terribly afraid." The Living Bible says "they were badly frightened." Clarence Jordan in *The Cotton Patch Version* says "it nearly scared the life out of them." The King James Version says "they were sore afraid." No matter how you slice it, this does not seem like a very good beginning for the Prince of Peace.

It was not just the presence of the angel that frightened the shepherds. It was all that light! The glory (literally, very apparent presence) of the Lord shone around them. What had been dark was turned to light. What had been nighttime had become daytime. God has a way of doing that! God has a way of transforming our despair into joy, our sin into righteousness, our scatteredness into wholeness. But that renovation of self is frightening. We wonder: *What will happen next?* We anticipate: *Will people still like me?* We think: *Am I strong enough for tomorrow?* The light of God's presence can be frightening.

But having seen the excitement and vigor of the sudden appearance of the angel and having learned the power of the message, let us not forget that this all occurred in the midst of routine life. It all started like any other night. As the familiar words of the King James Version report: "And there were in the same country shepherds abiding in the field, keeping watch over their flock by night"—just as they had done the night before and the night before that. The conversation that holy night did not begin, "Let us go now to Bethlehem and see this thing that has taken place." No, their conversation was probably more like: "Hey, Ralph, did you hear that they caught the guy who has been stealing sheep over in Bethany?" "Say, Bill, did you ever get a date with that waitress in Salim?" It would have been ordinary conversation among ordinary men.

It began in the midst of life's routine. I don't know about you, but I have more ordinary days than I do special days. There are more days when I just go about my usual things and fewer days of glitter and glamour. The good news is that God breaks through and uses the routine as the scene of God's activity.

Where was Martin Luther when he began to wrestle with the biblical truth that we are saved by grace through faith and not by good works? Luther was just doing his job as a professor, preparing a few lectures on Romans. It was routine, but God used it.

Where was John Wesley when he felt his heart strangely warmed and gained new assurance of Christ in his life? Wesley was at a regular prayer meeting on Aldersgate Street, noting in his journal that "I went unwillingly." It was routine, but God used it.

I got a note thanking me for something I said in a sermon. I did not even remember having said it. It was routine, but God used it. A clerk smiles instead of frowning. It is routine, but God uses it. A student is friendly to a newcomer. It is routine, but God uses it. A homebound member prays daily for the church. It is routine, but God uses it.

What a remarkable discovery! Every moment is a possibility for God. Every relationship is a potential for God. Every routine is an arena in which God can appear. What a gift it is, because now life can be lived on the tiptoe of expectancy. God takes life's routine as the crucible in which God mixes the good news.

The account of the shepherds begins with routine and breaks into jubilee. The host of angels sang, "Glory to God in the highest heaven, and on earth peace among those whom he favors." This gift is a universal gift: "highest heaven" and "earth" would be parallel terms that would cover the full universe. "Those whom he favors" would be all toward whom God extends grace; would that not include everyone?

After the angels went away, the shepherds decide to check out what has been told them. Reading that text (Luke 2:15) reminded me of an experience I had with a youth puppet team. We left our church and drove about an hour to give a program at the state prison for women. We all felt a little nervous when the series of gates and doors all clanged shut behind us. After setting up the puppet stage, all of the puppeteers were hidden behind the big curtain. We heard (but could not see) the women as they began to come in for the puppet show. Our puppet players were curious to see their audience, but the performers had to stay out of sight. We listened as folding chairs scraped and creaked as the women from the prison took their seats, and we got more edgy. Our youthful team members looked at one another in dismay as a gruff voice shuffled to a seat and said roughly, "This had better be good."

Was that the attitude of the shepherds who made their quick way to Bethlehem? "This had better be good." After all, they were risking leaving the sheep to go see what had been told them by some unusual night visitors. What attitude do we bring to the manger? Looking for proof? Looking for peace? Looking for purpose?

It was as had been told them. God keeps God's promises! And the shepherds "made known" (Luke 2:17) what the Lord had "made known" (Luke 2:15) to them. Interestingly, Luke uses two different words for "made known." The word for "which the Lord has *made known* to us" means "helped us understand." The word for "they *made known* what had been told them" means "inscribed knowledge" or "spread the word." The first has a sense of revelation; the second has a sense of sharing the news. That's not a bad rhythm for those who meet Jesus!

Those who remembered Micah 5:2 would not be surprised to find this birth in Bethlehem:

> But you, O Bethlehem of Ephrathah,
>> who are one of the little clans of Judah,
> from you shall come forth for me
>> one who is to rule in Israel,
> whose origin is from of old,
>> from ancient days.

Those who remembered 1 Samuel 16:11 would not be surprised to find shepherds near Bethlehem, the city of David ("[David] is keeping the sheep"). Shepherds and Bethlehem and the Savior's birth seem to go together.

Although the text only mentions Mary, Joseph, the baby, and the shepherds, there must have been some other people around. The birth is near an inn and that is a public place. Bethlehem was a small enough town that word of a new baby would get around rather quickly. Luke 2:17-18 implies that the shepherds spoke to people who might not have known the significance of this birth. Mary and Joseph would have known, even if the implication of that knowledge was not clear. (Mary had been told this child would be called "Son of God"—Luke 1:35. In Matthew's account, 1:20-21, Joseph is counseled that the child would be a savior.)

In Luke's telling of the story, the people to whom the shepherds spoke were "amazed" at what they were told. This does not mean that they believed it. In fact, the King James Version reports that "they wondered." This could be an awed wonder, or it could be an "I don't get it" wonder. In the New Testament language, the root word means "to look closely." To me, that sounds as if some of these people wanted to give the whole matter a second look. Hearing the good news is not the same thing as accepting the good news.

What do we know about how some of those present responded to the baby Jesus? In this account from Luke, there are two responses to the birth of Christ: Mary's response and the shepherds' response. It's not that one is right and the other wrong; it's just that they are different. Mary kept these words, pondering them in her heart (Luke 2:19). The shepherds "made known what had been told them about this child," and "returned, glorifying and praising God for all they had heard and seen" (Luke 2:17, 20). There are two ways of responding: pondering and proclaiming.

We don't do much pondering these days. We are a more action-oriented society. Someone asked a man, "What do you do for a living?" The man answered, "I am a philosopher." "Yeah," his questioner continued, "but what do you *do?*" Isn't that the way we greet newcomers: "What do you do?" (In fact, are we pressing the point to note that we exchange pleasantries by asking—without meaning it!—"How do you do?")

Mary had a while to reflect on this strange gift in her life. From the time the angel visited her to this moment in the stable, she had considered all this. All that time—nine months, if my figuring is correct. Maybe that's why we do not ponder, reflect, and consider. It just takes too long!

But not too long for Jesus, who in the final days of his life went to a garden for some time apart. But not for Martin Luther, who is reputed to have said, "I have so much to do today that I must pray for at least five hours." But not for Mary, who kept all these things, who kept these words, and pondered them in her heart.

The word translated "pondered" (*sumballō*) literally means "to throw all together." Pondering means thinking about all of the possibilities. Pondering means leaving old answers, to return only if the new answers do not work. Pondering means stepping to tomorrow instead of jumping to conclusions. Mary pondered these words in her heart.

I imagine she was wondering what it would mean for her child to be Messiah. Did the nails of Calvary begin to prick the hand of her newborn? I imagine she was wondering what it would be like to be parent to the Son of God. Did the awesome responsibility of shaping a young life begin to gnaw at her? I imagine she was wondering what reaction Nazareth might give her and Joseph (and the baby) if they returned there after the strange story of how this child was conceived. Would the people of the village come and worship or come and sneer? It is not a surprise that Mary pondered these things!

We sing "Go, Tell It on the Mountain"—yes, but there is a place for the quiet, reflective spirit.

We sing "We've a Story to Tell to the Nations"—yes, but some of us are given the grace for patient waiting more than we've been given the gifts for talking and telling.

We sing "Reach the world"—yes, but such a journey begins in the starting place of one's inner being.

Some of us have been given the heart and mind for reflection and quiet and wonderment, but somehow we have thought that "pondering" meant a second-class faith.

We are tempted to think that really faithful people always have to act and do and speak. Not so for Mary! There was always a sense of "I don't quite understand" in Mary's view of Jesus. But that gift of mystery and bewilderment is a gift from God.

Maybe Christmas is not really a time for saying, "Oh, yeah, I understand." Maybe it is a time to say no more than, "I come to worship. Mystery! Grace! Pondering!" Thank you, Mary.

Then, the shepherds. If Mary responded by pondering, the shepherds responded by proclaiming. These hillside heroes dared to go they knew not where to see this baby that they knew not fully. But, boy, when they left! Glorifying! Praising! Here is another side of Christmas—pondering, yes, but also proclaiming.

Maybe it is not for all of us, but it is surely for some of us. The Charles Schulz comic strip *Peanuts* has often included some delightful reminders of the heartbeat of Christmas. One time, all week before Christmas, Lucy was practicing her line in the Christmas play. She was to step onto the stage and in her best angel voice say, "Hark!" All week she worked on it, saying it with just the right profundity. The night of the play came. She stepped onto the stage, and in her best angel voice she said—"Hockey stick!"

I don't know what the shepherds said when they returned, but—"hockey stick" or "hark"—it was a word of joy and praise. The word may not be perfect, but let the message be clear: "Boy, have I got good news for you!"

That is the response to being in the presence of Christ Jesus—to proclaim fully and freely that this is Lord and Savior.

Someone proclaimed that word to you; someone proclaimed that word to me, someone who by life or word has said to us that there is victory to be found in the Bethlehem manger. God does not leave God's presence without a witness among us. Be it saint or be it stone, be it family or be it friend, be it who we are or where we are, the Spirit of God finds vehicles for the word that God is love.

A Time with Young Disciples

On Christmas Eve, children (and those parents who have not yet followed the "easy assembly" steps for the new bicycle) are usually very excited. This service might be one in which children are invited into leadership roles.

Children could serve as greeters and as ushers. (The youngest ones might feel more comfortable if there is an adult companion close by.) If the service is an informal one at which refreshments are served, some children could help give out "the goodies." If the service is one where the Lord's Supper is celebrated, could older children help the pastor serve the elements? How about having a child read the traditional Christmas Scripture lessons? Is there a child who would offer a prayer as part of this worship experience? If you are having a candlelight service, can children distribute the candles? An older child can be acolyte to light the services. (If there has been an Advent wreath—see "Advent Wreath" below—be sure the acolyte understands to light the Christ candle as well as the four Advent candles.)

Family travel schedules might make it difficult to have a full children's choir (at the church I attend, "full" would mean three or four children) but special music could include children, either singing as a group or as soloists. Children often enjoy teaching grown-ups a hymn or praise chorus they have learned. (That's not a bad way to get some new music into the congregation's repertoire!) In singing a familiar carol ("Silent Night," for example), divide the hymn so that adult men sing one stanza, adult women sing another stanza, children sing another stanza, and all sing some of the stanzas. (Be careful not to word this in such a way that youth feel left out!)

Some congregations have a tradition of a children's Christmas pageant on Christmas Eve. You could have children act the roles in the story told on pages 46-48 ("Fourth Sunday of Advent"). Have the children practice several times how they might demonstrate what is going on in the story. (For example, how would an uncle and his nephew look the first time they go together to watch over the sheep—nervous? proud? uncertain? pleased? How could one show that emotion?) At the service, read the story slowly as the children respond to the account. (Most of the children will enjoy showing how the shepherds looked when they were terrified at the sudden light and the appearance of the angel.) The story closes with a smile on the face of Jesus. Ask the children: "How would you look if Jesus smiled at you?"

At Christmas Eve services, families often want to sit together. Children who would be in a child-care room for other services will be at the Christmas Eve service. Would crayons and appropriate coloring pages help the youngest ones stay engaged? Would "children's Bibles" with pictures help boys and girls follow the scriptures? Some congregations have "family friendly" services in the late afternoon of December 24 and typically do not expect young children at a late evening service ("visions of sugar plums" and all that). If there is a "nursery" available during the Christmas Eve service, there may be times when these children might be invited to come to the worship space for special parts of the service. (In some congregations, younger children are regularly brought from the nursery when it is time to take Communion.)

Hymns

Although the music has been playing for weeks in malls and on radio broadcasts and television specials, most congregants will want to sing traditional Christmas carols at the Christmas Eve service. (I still remember going out into a city street, where police had blocked traffic, and joining an urban congregation as worshipers held lighted candles and sang "Silent Night, Holy Night."

Passersby stopped and joined in. It was as if the angel's word to the shepherds was being fulfilled: this birth was for "all the people.")

There are some other, less familiar, Christmas hymns. Look through sources for different ways of singing about the babe in Bethlehem. The African American spiritual "Rise Up, Shepherd, and Follow" offers an invitation to go to Bethlehem. "One Holy Night in Bethlehem" retells the story of Christ's birth through the eyes of shepherds, of Mary, of Joseph, and of ourselves. "Joseph Dearest, Joseph Mine" is a traditional song from Europe; it helps us see Joseph moving into his parenting role. "Light of the World" and "This Is Christmas" are two contemporary interpretations of the birth of our Lord. Although not specifically about Christmas, "Love Is Here" is a contemporary chorus that resonates with the theme of "the birth of love."

The refrain from "Angels We Have Heard on High" (found in most hymnals; hymn 238 in *The United Methodist Hymnal*) is known by many congregations. The words are vigorously sung: "Gloria, in excelsis Deo!"—Glory to God in the highest. Consider using that refrain as a sung response throughout the service: after the call to worship, after the opening hymn, after the congregational/pastoral prayer, in the midst of the Gospel lesson—Luke 2:14—and at the close of the reading of the text, as a prayer of thanksgiving after receiving the Lord's Supper, and at the close of the service. (You know how it is—with any luck, that refrain will get stuck in people's heads and they will end up humming, whistling, and singing it all day long on Christmas Day!)

Advent Wreath

Invite five persons who represent the variety of your congregation to light the candles. For example, as the "one voice" begins the responsive reading, a child might light the first candle; someone with ethnic heritage different from most of the congregation could light the second candle; a single mom could light the third candle; a youth could light the fourth candle; and one of the oldest members of the congregation could light the Christ candle.

One Voice:	The journey began in Nazareth.
All Voices:	**Mary, you will have a son.**
One Voice:	The journey continued to Bethlehem.
All Voices:	**There is no room at the inn.**
One Voice:	The journey continued to a field of shepherds.
All Voices:	**I am bringing you good news of great joy for all the people.**
One Voice:	The journey continued to a manger.
All Voices:	**And he shall be called the Son of God.**
One Voice:	The journey is a journey of light.
All Voices:	**And now the Light is here!**
One Voice:	And it is the Light of the World!
All Voices:	**Amen! Amen! Amen!**

Have You Thought of Doing This?

Christmas is, in some ways, the most painful holiday for persons who feel alone. Perhaps they recall happier times or earlier family days or when a loved one was with them or simply when they had a place to call home. It is difficult to be in a culture that shouts "I'll Be Home for Christmas" when home seems empty or, for some, nonexistent.

Offer a Christmas meal before or after the Christmas Eve service. It is not to be aimed at those families who already have too much to do or those persons who have bountiful and beautiful relationships. The meal will be a gift to those for whom there is no room at the inn of their lives. You could even put a sign-up sheet in some local gathering places. Or you might do a cooperative program with a local shelter.

Spread the word through the homeless community. Most pastors know one or two persons who regularly come to the church for help. Could these persons take the word into the shelters, the streets, the underpasses where the homeless live? A clearly identified church van could go to areas where homeless persons tend to gather; invite them to come to the church. Of course, this will seem risky to some of the homeless. Would it be better in your setting to take the food to the homeless instead of having them come to the church?

There are others who will be alone at Christmas. Is there a student from another country who cannot get back home for the holidays? (Check with nearby colleges.) Is there someone whose family is far away or whose close relatives have died or whose familial relations are severed? Invite him or her for a meal. If it does not seem feasible to have a Christmas Eve meal at the church, link church families with those who are alone at Christmas. ("Mrs. Brown, I hope you'll come and have dinner with us on Christmas Eve.")

Children sometimes are overwhelmed by the fever-pitch pace of Christmas. Children who are living in homeless shelters or "safe shelters" (for escaping family abuse) may feel they are less than their peers "who seem to have everything." A Christmas Eve party for these children could restore their sense of being in a balanced world. (Perhaps, a portly gentleman in a red suit could squeeze in a visit for this occasion.)

Of course, it is not easy to get church volunteers to do much volunteering when their own Christmas calendars are so packed. Nevertheless, what a few can do in the name of the Body of Christ may well be the only trip to the manger that some in the community will have.

AN UNLIKELY
CHRISTMAS CARD

Question: Is death part of Christmas?
A Thought: Jesus touches every part of life and death.

Scripture: *Matthew 2:13-23*

Now after they had left, an angel of the Lord appeared to Joseph in a dream, and said, "Get up, take the child and his mother, and flee to Egypt, and remain there until I tell you; for Herod is about to search for the child, to destroy him." Then Joseph got up, took the child and his mother by night, and went to Egypt, and remained there until the death of Herod. This was to fulfill what had been spoken by the Lord through the prophet, "Out of Egypt I have called my son."

When Herod saw that he had been tricked by the wise men, he was infuriated, and he sent and killed all the children in and around Bethlehem who were two years old or under, according to the time that he had learned from the wise men. Then was fulfilled what had been spoken through the prophet Jeremiah:

"A voice was heard in Ramah,
   wailing and loud lamentation,
Rachel weeping for her children;
   she refused to be consoled, because they are no more."

When Herod died, an angel of the Lord suddenly appeared in a dream to Joseph in Egypt and said, "Get up, take the child and his mother, and go to the land of Israel. . . ." But when he heard that Archelaus was ruling over Judea in place of his father Herod, he was afraid to go there. And after being warned in a dream, he went away to the district of Galilee. There he made his home in a town called Nazareth, so that what had been spoken through the prophets might be fulfilled, "He will be called a Nazorean."

Call to Worship

One Voice: Christ is born; give him glory! (English)

All Voices: Cristo ha nacido; dar gloria! (Spanish)

One Voice: Le Christ est né, lui donner la gloire! (French)

All Voices: Christus ist geboren; ihm Ehre! (German)

One Voice: Kristo ay ipinanganak; magbigay ng kaluwalhatian sa kanya! (Tagalog)

All Voices: Kristus er fodt; give ham herlighed! (Danish)

One Voice: Around the world, we gather to praise God for the One who was sent to save the people.

All Voices: O come, let us adore him, Christ the Lord!

Pastoral Prayer

(Note in the bulletin or project on the screen that the leader will invite the congregation to respond from time to time by saying together "**Amen.**")

Dear Lord Jesus, words cannot contain the joy that bursts within us as we smile at your manger. As the prophets have promised, you have been born, and now year after year after year after year, we celebrate that you have been born in the hearts of your people. And all of God's people said together: **Amen.**

Gracious triune God, there has never been a time when you were not, but by your good favor you chose to be a living Word among us, a Word become flesh; and we receive, accept, and enjoy that gift in Jesus. As Mary and Joseph said *yes* to your plan, without always knowing where it would lead, so we offer our *yes*, however pale, as a beginning of our service from this Christmas Day. And all of God's people said together: **Amen.**

Your journey, dear Lord, from Bethlehem to (*name the community where you are*), has touched places of threat, places of pain, and a place of death. Even as we are reminded of the diverse steps for our own journeys, remind us too of your living presence to walk with us. Your living presence is a loving presence, and we are grateful. And all of God's people said together: **Amen.**

We confess that we should really like to stay in the glad moment of Christmas, to linger with you in places where angels sing and shepherds praise and mother love is gentle and sweet. But when we do that, Holy One, we do not go where you go, to places of hunger, to places of loneliness, to places of war, to places of despair, to places of injustice. Hear our confession as an openness to walk with you as fully as you walk with us. And all of God's people said together: **Amen.**

(*Here the one leading the prayer may include confessions, petitions, intercessions, and thanksgivings appropriate to the community.*)

Finally, we come as you taught us, praying as you taught us, "Our Father . . ."

Some Ingredients to Stir into the Sermon Pot

Not Sweetness, but a Shocking Thriller

Isn't it funny how Egypt keeps popping up in the biblical story of God's people? First, it is a place of captivity, as Joseph is sent there by slave-traders (Genesis 37:36). Then, when there was a famine elsewhere, Egypt became a place of refuge and a source of food (Genesis 42:1-2). Next, Israelites found Egypt as a good place to raise a family, so many of them moved there and prospered (Exodus 1:1-7). New leadership in Egypt saw all the Israelites as competition, so the king ordered the Hebrews into slavery (Exodus 1:8-14). Finally—after four hundred thirty years—the children of Israel began their escape from the slavery of Egypt (Exodus 12:40-42). Then, with great irony, when Mary and Joseph had to escape the evil pursuit made by Herod, they were inspired to take their child and go to Egypt, a place of safety (Matthew 2:13-15). The next step—in the account of the holy family—is a return home from Egypt, this time not as escaping slaves, as generations earlier had done, but as persons simply ready to get home (Matthew 2:19-23) in order to move ahead with God's plan.

How old was Jesus when the family left for Egypt? How long did they stay in Egypt? Scholars do not agree. Some note that if Herod wanted all male babies under two killed, he must have anticipated that Jesus would have been somewhere in that age range. How old was Jesus when the wise men arrived? Did the family stay in Bethlehem for a year or more? The Bible does not speak to this point. If they did, and if they stayed in the stable, we have to give an A+ in hospitality to the innkeeper!

They were in Egypt until Herod died (Matthew 2:19). Historians report that Herod died in 4 BCE (remember that calendars have changed; "4 BCE" does not mean that Herod died before Jesus was born!). Was that a year later? Four years later? How long would it have taken for word to get to Egypt that Herod had died back in Judea? How long would it have taken for the holy family to make the trek from Egypt to Judea? (If this is the same donkey that carried Mary from Nazareth to Bethlehem, this would be one tired donkey!) Matthew does not think these kinds of details (that so fascinate us) are important. God's revelation to Matthew does not chase what one writer called "skinny rabbits."

The story of the escape to Egypt by Mary, Joseph, and the child is a far cry from the sweetness of our Christmas cards. It is not a pretty scene, and it is one we usually leave out of our Yuletide memories. "The Massacre of the Innocents," as it is sometimes called, is not the stuff of church pageants. But there is a power in this part of the story that can enrich us, sustain us, encourage us, and, finally, free us. It's the sort of work that Christ came to do!

The power is the truth that God lives in the same world as we do. This is not a remote divinity, one who knows nothing of and cares little about our human situation. This is the holy One who lives in a world where despots are threatened by a little child, where violence and murder are seen as the solution to differences, and where good people have to travel under the cover of darkness in order to be safe. Christmas means nothing if it cannot be true in a world of Herods. Christmas means nothing if

God's plan can be spoiled by evil plots. Christmas means nothing if Christ comes only to places where all is well.

But Christmas *does* have meaning, because its gift of love is real even in a world of Herods. But Christmas *does* have meaning, because God's plan is not spoiled by evil plots. But Christmas *does* have meaning, because Christ comes to live in the kind of world in which we live. Christmas is both happy, joyful carols *and* the weeping of Rachel, who, the text says, cried for her children, now gone. Matthew 2:13-23 reminds us of that.

We know that the story ends up with Jesus and his family returning to "the old country." But, if we did not know that, these verses would unfold as a murder mystery thriller. How is this for the plot of a television program? Important visitors leave (Matthew 2:13). There is a warning of trouble (Matthew 2:13). There is a message to "run for your lives" (Matthew 2:13). The evil protagonist is identified (Matthew 2:13). The family slip off to a foreign country, traveling only at night (Matthew 2:14). Word comes that a prophet had said all this would happen (Matthew 2:15). The evildoer realizes that he has been duped (Matthew 2:16). In his fury, he sets out to wipe out any child who might be the one he really wants to kill, so, just in case the one he wants is in disguise, he murders all male children two years old and younger (Matthew 2:16). Word comes that this kind of thing might have been expected (Matthew 2:17-18). The evil king dies (Matthew 2:19). The family gets a message that it is okay to return home (Matthew 2:20). But about the time they think it is safe, they learn that the son of the evil king is now in charge (Matthew 2:23). Finally, the three—Mary, Joseph, Jesus—make it back to hometown Nazareth (Matthew 2:23). This saga has all the elements needed for an exciting drama: a roller coaster of emotions, the threat and reality of evildoing, and false endings followed by a happy ending. Whew! Try putting all that in your annual Christmas letter!

Who was this Herod? He was appointed by Julius Caesar to be governor of Galilee. He was promoted by having Syria added to his territory. Before long, he was named king of Judea. Although Herod was not a very observant Jew, he did a few things that helped the Jewish people. For example, he did not put his image on coins so Jews were free to use the coins without violating the prohibition about graven images. By giving some generous bribes, he also kept the Romans from desecrating the temple in Jerusalem. His method of stabilizing the government was to kill anyone who got in his way. He ruled for thirty-three years and as his life and reign moved toward the end, he became quite ill. Some accounts even say worms were eating away his body. How tormenting this must have been for a man who once had been a prime athlete.

Herod was still a jealous and prideful man. He was so concerned that there might not be sufficient mourners at his funeral that he ordered that the seventy religious leaders be killed when he died. That ought to create some mourning! When Herod died, his sister lied and said he had changed his mind about the killings, so the lives of the leaders were spared.

It is not surprising, given Herod's fear of competition (King of the Jews, indeed!) and in light of the ease with which he killed, that he ordered the death of the youngest children of Bethlehem. Probably about thirty to forty died in that slaughter. (Some secular historians note that there seems to be no collaborating evidence that this tragedy took place, but Bethlehem was not a place of much import in the Roman empire, so it is quite possible that no officials took note of the matter.)

In Matthew 2:13, when Joseph gets instructions in a dream "to flee," there is more impact to the word "flee" than simply "get out of town." The New Testament word also carries with it the implication of rushing in order to get away from something, to leave in order to shun (or escape) something. That is clearly what Joseph, Mary, and Jesus did.

Because the evil of Herod seems so heinous, we are likely to assume that we personally do not have the ingredients for such sin. But we do. It is when we call our evil "good." Albert Camus wrote, "If you can explain evil successfully, you stop your fight against it." Remember Eve? She took of the forbidden fruit in the Garden not in order to embarrass God but because it could do something good for her. Genesis 3:6 says, "When the woman saw that the tree was good for food, and that it was a delight to the eyes, and that the tree was to be desired to make one wise, she took of its fruit and ate." At the core (no pun intended!) of this first brokenness from God was the foolishness of calling "good" something that was wrong.

It is easy to name evils as goods. In Friedrich Durrenmatt's play *The Visit*, Claire returns to her German hometown and offers 500,000,000 marks to the dying town and 500,000,000 marks to be divided evenly among the townspeople if they will kill a man who wronged her years ago. "No!" they said. "This is wrong!"

Later, they decide that "justice should be done." The burgomaster says, "Then, I proceed to the vote. All those who are in accord with the terms of this gift will signify the same by raising their right hands. All against? The offer is accepted. I now solemnly call upon you, fellow townsmen, to declare in the face of all the world that you take this action not out of love for worldly gain, but out of love for the right. We join together as brothers . . . to purify our town of guilt . . . and to reaffirm our faith . . . in the eternal power of justice." (Patrick Bowles, trans. [London: Jonathan Cape, 1962].) The lights go out in the room and the man is killed. Evil is called good.

Evil is called good sometimes in the church. We have cliques and call it fellowship. We ignore the lessons of the past and call it keeping up-to-date. We resist growing spiritually and call it remembering our heritage.

But Matthew is still telling a Merry Christmas story. It is still good news because the story is about the one named Jesus, whose name means "shall save." This is he who "will save his people from their sins" (Matthew 1:21). Herod does not win, nor do the evil forces of our day, even those that fester in our own hearts. Christmas is for real because it outlives the Herods of the world. Christmas is for real because we do not have to pretend about being perfect; the babe of Bethlehem came into an imperfect world—like the one in which we live and participate—and there is an empty tomb that says, "Death, you gave it your best shot and still Jesus has won."

Finally, even the account of the escape to Egypt and the murder of boys of Bethlehem are not the chronicles of Herod's life. These strange verses in Matthew 2:13-23 are the narratives of the life of Jesus. For all of his puff and pageantry, Herod is not the reason for remembering these events. As the seasonal cliché says: "Jesus is the reason for the season." We remember this painful, angry story because it reminds us that God's love is for just such a world.

Three times Matthew tells us that these experiences "fulfill" God's plan (Matthew 2:15, 17, 23). That does not mean that God intended for children to be murdered; it means that God's plan included a world where such horrible things could happen. God was not oblivious to the world into which God was sending the Son of God. In these three verses, Matthew uses three different words that are often translated "fulfill." The words he uses are words that describe what has happened when a deep hole is filled or when an empty net is crammed full. That is the fulfillment that comes with this Christmas Day: the gracious and free love from God has come to enter the empty places of our lives, to fill them with hope and joy and wholeness. That is why we can say "Merry Christmas!"

A Time with Young Disciples

If Christmas Day has come on Sunday, the children who are present may be tired and upset at having to leave the treasures of Christmas morning at home. Perhaps—if you are a person of great courage!—you could invite the children to talk about how they feel about "having to come to church." The bottom line is that many of them will resent having to be there, but they will understand why the service is being held. In some ways, it will be even more difficult for children to attend a Christmas Day service if it does not fall on a Sunday (or whenever the congregation worships regularly).

Be sensitive to the fact that Christmas will not feel the same way in every home represented among the boys and girls. Some may be from single-parent homes where the absence of the other parent is magnified at Christmas. Some children will dread the inevitable "what did you get for Christmas" comparing ritual among their peers. Some children will bring major disappointment about a gift they had expected but did not receive. Some are not looking forward to a traditional family trip. (That distaste for the family event could have sinister implications—for example, seeing again an uncle or cousin who has been sexually abusive with the child.) Some children will be visitors on a holiday excursion that has taken them away from familiar surroundings.

Awareness of these negative possibilities may keep us from a well-meaning way of saying things that could actually be hurtful. Having mentioned all that, I do not mean that we should make Christmas Day a downer. On the contrary! If appropriate, you could point out that the cloth hangings (the paraments) are now white or gold. White fabric and gold cloth are used in many cultures to represent joy. Ask: What are some other ways we show joy and happiness? (Singing. Laughing. Playing. Smiling. Helping.) Why do we sing "Joy to the World"? (Because the Lord has come—because Jesus is born.)

Some congregations have a custom of celebrating Jesus' birthday by having a birthday cake for Jesus, and even singing "Happy Birthday" to our Lord. This has the danger of trivializing the sacred gift, but it also has the potential of expanding how we understand the meaning of his birth. Use a marker to print on a large sheet of paper how persons might say "Happy birthday, Jesus!" in various languages. Let the children try to pronounce these greetings. If you have persons who can help with the correct pronunciation, so much the better! Use the multilingual birthday greetings as a transition to talking about the universal love of God seen in Jesus.

Here are some ways to say "Happy birthday, Jesus" in various languages:

Joyeux anniversaire, Jesus! (French)
¡Feliz cumpleaños, Jesús! (Spanish)
Chúc mừng sinh nhật Jesus! (Vietnamese)
shēngrì kuàilè, Jesus (Chinese)
Wszystkiego najlepszego z okazji urodzin, Jezu! (Polish)
Nakutakia mema kwa siku yako ya kuzaliwa!, Jesu! (Swahili)

Alles Gute zum Geburtstag, Jesus! (German)

Another idea: Get a calendar for next year. Show how many days there are until Christmas next year. If some of the children like to count, ask them to count the days. Older children could add up the number of days in the months. Then comment: "That is a long time away! What can we do to remember this Christmas until next year?" (Serving others, coming to church, thinking of Jesus, praying, reading the Bible, Holy Communion.) How can we start getting ready for next Christmas? (Someone may say, "Do our shopping early," but others will suddenly realize that we prepare for next Christmas in the same ways we remember this Christmas: serving others, coming to church, thinking of Jesus, praying, reading the Bible, Holy Communion.)

Hymns

Check the hymnbook your congregation most frequently uses. (If you do not use hymnals, find a resource that will help you apply this to your setting.) Go to the section that includes hymns for Christmas. (In the hymnal in front of me, that portion is a subsection called "Birth and Baptism," which is part of a larger section called "Christ's Gracious Life.") At the bottom of the page (or, in some hymnals, at the top) you will likely find the name of the person who wrote the words and the source of the music. (There are reference books such as *The Companion to The United Methodist Hymnal* and *Hymnal Companion to the Lutheran Book of Worship* that will give you information about these writers and musicians.) Go through the Christmas hymns. From what country do they come? For example, this is what I found as the backgrounds of the Christmas hymns in one hymnal:

Words: Unknown	Music: United States
Words: United States	Music: United States
Words: England	Music: England
Words: Scotland	Music: England
Words: England	Music: England

Words: Venezuela	Music: Venezuela
Words: Germany	Music: Germany
Words: Latin	Music: Germany
Words: Scripture	Music: United States
Words: France	Music: France
Words: France	Music: France
Words: Poland	Music: Poland
Words: United States	Music: United States
Words: Unknown	Music: Germany
Words: Spain	Music: Spain
Words: France	Music: France
Words: Czech Republic	Music: Czech Republic
Words: Ireland	Music: England
Words: France	Music: France
Words: France	Music: France
Words: Austria	Music: Austria
Words: England	Music: Germany
Words: Scotland	Music: Malawi
Words: England	Music: Ireland
Words: Puerto Rico	Music: Puerto Rico
Words: Canada	Music: Canada
Words: England	Music: England
Words: England	Music: England
Words: Germany	Music: Germany
Words: Latin	Music: England
Words: United States	Music: United States
Words: England	Music: England
Words: African American	Music: African American

Include in your service notes (printed or projected) information about the hymns being sung. Point out the range of nations represented in the hymnbook. (This is one sign of the universal nature of God's love.) If there is an unfamiliar Christmas hymn you have been itching to sing, arrange for the children to learn it. On this Christmas Day service, get the children to "teach" it to the choir. Then the choir can help the children teach it to the congregation. There is a good chance that the Christmas Day service will unfold informally, so this kind of casual singing just might fit the order of the day!

Advent Wreath

Arrange for someone to light "everything in sight"! Wait until all the candles are lit before beginning this litany.

One Voice: Christmas! The full Light of God is among us.
All Voices: Noel! Noel! The news is good!
One Voice: In the midst of the world's night, the morning breaks in bright array!
All Voices: Noel! Noel! The news is good!
One Voice: Love's pure Light shines forever.
All Voices: Noel! Noel! The news is good!
One Voice: Noel!
All Voices: Noel!
One Voice: The news is good!
All Voices: Thank God! The news is good!

Have You Thought of Doing This?

What are ways that the congregation can make a public celebration of the good news of Christmas?

1. Include words and pictures of joy on the congregation's Web site or Facebook page. Take out an ad in a local newspaper, not to advertise church activities but simply to offer public praise to God.
2. Put large wreaths on the most visible outside doors of the church building.
3. If you have had a nativity scene display, make a huge sign that reads "Noel!" and put that sign over the top of the nativity scene.
4. If special flowers have been used (some churches have poinsettias), place these flowers on the front steps of the church. If persons take these flowers—thinking they are stealing them—they might be surprised to find a note saying, "This flower is given to you by (*name of church*) to help you celebrate the birth of Christ."

5. If you have a bell, ring it as the congregation gathers.
6. If you have a carillon or amplification system, offer the community a gift of Christmas music.
7. After the service, make special visits to nursing homes and homeless shelters to bring Christmas greetings.
8. Invite the children and youth of the church to use sidewalk chalk to write words of Christmas greeting and pictures of the Christmas story on any pavement around the church.
9. Offer a living nativity scene. (The characters of the Christmas story are represented by persons who typically dress in first-century clothing. They form the picture of the stable in Bethlehem and hold their position "frozen." (Stretch breaks are needed!) A contemporary alternative might be to have the living nativity scene but have Mary, Joseph, the shepherds, et al., dressed in contemporary clothing.
10. Hang a gigantic banner across the main entrance to the church building or meeting space. The banner could simply have the word "Noel."
11. Have a Christmas parade (in some places you will need a parade permit to do this). March in procession on the streets of your community, carrying Christmas banners, signs, and symbols. (Is there someone who could make a Chrismon that is three feet high?) If your gathering place is not near major streets, could you team with another (more visible) congregation to do a parade together?
12. Ask the Christmas Day congregation to stand outside in front of the church's gathering place to sing Christmas carols.
13. To those who attend the Christmas Day service, give cards (probably produced with your computer and printer) that read: "On Christmas Day, I worshiped at (*name of church*). We celebrated the birth of Jesus. Can I tell you about it?" Include an address and phone number and/or Web site for the church. Persons can distribute the cards when it seems appropriate (while respecting the privacy, dignity, and beliefs of others).

14. If your church is located where there are passersby or where there is room for persons to stop and stare, do a mime enactment of the Christmas story. It will take some practicing, but act out the Christmas story without using any words. Do the "performance" (probably repeating it several times) where onlookers can watch. Have a sign asking "What are we doing?" Visitors could make their guesses to a designated listener. It would be delightful for the listener to keep a record of what was said and to share this with the congregation later. Include a large sign that says, "If you want to know more . . ." and have someone at the sign to distribute copies of the New Testament.

JOHN THE BAPTIZER: JESUS' UNLIKELY HERALD

Question: Who tells others about Christ?
A *Thought*: John the Baptizer is pointing in the right direction.

Scripture: John 1:1-14

In the beginning was the Word, and the Word was with God, and the Word was God. He was in the beginning with God. All things came into being through him, and without him not one thing came into being. What has come into being in him was life, and the life was the light of all people. The light shines in the darkness, and the darkness did not overcome it.

There was a man sent from God, whose name was John. He came as a witness to testify to the light, so that all might believe through him. He himself was not the light, but he came to testify to the light. The true light, which enlightens everyone, was coming into the world.

He was in the world, and the world came into being through him; yet the world did not know him. He came to what was his own, and his own people did not accept him. But to all who received him, who believed in his name, he gave power to become children of God, who were born, not of blood or of the will of the flesh or of the will of man, but of God.

And the Word became flesh and lived among us, and we have seen his glory, the glory as of a father's only son, full of grace and truth.

Call to Worship

One Voice: Why do we come this day?

All Voices: We have seen a light.

One Voice: For whom has this light come?

All Voices: The light is a light for all people.

One Voice: How then shall others see the light?

All Voices: We shall testify and tell of the light we have seen.

One Voice: Come then; let us worship the Light that has become flesh and lived in our midst.

All Voices: Christ is the world's light, Christ and none other! Glory to God on high! (This line is based on a hymn by Fred Pratt Green, "Christ Is the World's Light," hymn 188 in *The United Methodist Hymnal*.)

Pastoral Prayer

As we move into the New Year, O Lord, you have moved ahead of us and now meet us in these fresh calendar days. Out of the bounty of your Christmas gift from Bethlehem, you have brought Light into the world. Even in the midst of our human conflicts, the Light shines. Even in the midst of our inner struggles, the Light shines. Even in the midst of unjust systems, the Light shines. The darkness has not overcome it.

We give you thanks for the fullness of your endowment in Christ Jesus. Take now our thanksgiving and give it legs in our serving; take now our thanksgiving and give it arms in our testimony; take now our thanksgiving and give it life in our being. Our little flickers are not the light to which our thanksgiving points; rather, our serving, our testimony, our being all point to the Light that is for all people, the Light that invites everyone to claim, "I am a child of God!"

Light of the world, forgive us when we try to put *your* light under a bushel basket. Hear our confession that we try to run on batteries so that our light sometimes begins to fade. Instead, turn us as mirrors to reflect your light, even as we reflect your image in which we have been created. We have seen the glory of your Word, the glory as of a father's only son, full of grace and truth. Alleluia!

(Here the one leading the prayer may include petitions, intercessions, and thanksgivings appropriate to the community.)

Hear the prayer we dare to bring because even now your Light shines on your throne of grace, praying as you taught us, "Our Father . . ."

Some Ingredients to Stir into the Sermon Pot

Not Your Standard Wise Man

Epiphany is traditionally a season on which the church remembers the wise men who came to Bethlehem and offered gifts to the Christ child. Then, being warned in a dream not to get anywhere near King Herod, they returned home (back east) by a detour route (Matthew 2:1-12). Although January 6 is Epiphany Day, many congregations observe the day on the first Sunday after January 6. The word "epiphany" means "appearance," "manifestation," or "showing forth." At the heart of the celebration is a recognition that God in Christ has made an appearance to "all the world," including Gentiles such as the wise men.

The text recommended for this service (John 1:1-14) does not mention the wise men. It is about the Word that became flesh and lived among us and about a man sent by God to point toward that Word (John 1:6, 14). These verses from John are about God's "appearance, manifestation, and showing forth"—God's epiphany—in the Word, in the Light that lived among us. John the Baptizer is an unlikely choice to turn others toward the Christ, but one that the text says "was . . . sent from God." The word for "sent" is a word we recognize: *apŏstĕllō*—*apostle*. The definition carries with it an implication of being sent with a mission.

Why was John the Baptizer a good one to be a herald for the Christ? There is a clue in another place in John's (John, the evangelist) account: the Baptizer said, speaking of Christ, "He must increase, but I must decrease" (John 3:30). The willingness to prepare the way was a key to the Baptizer's effectiveness. There was a custom in ancient times of getting things ready if the king was about to visit: straighten out the curves in the road, lower the hills to make the road level, and smooth out the rough places (see Isaiah 40:3-4). That would make it easier for the king to arrive. The Baptizer did that for Jesus.

The Baptizer had no pretense at royal accoutrements. A palace? He lived in a cave. Rich foods? He ate wild honey and locusts. Handsome garments? He wore a cloak of scratchy camel hair. John the Baptizer never confused himself with his cousin Jesus (Luke 1:24, 39-40, 57, 63, 80). The Gospel according to John said it clearly: "He himself [John the Baptizer] was not the light, but he came to testify to the light."

Testify? In New Testament language, the word "testify" (or "witness") carries a strong connotation that we might miss in English. The Greek word is *martureō*. The word is first cousin to our English word "martyr." Testifying = martyrdom? Matthew 14:1-12 gives the sad chronicle of how John the Baptizer was put to death. Pointing to the Light of Christ, which sheds brightness upon what we would rather keep hidden—our lust, our deceit, our injustice—led to the death of the Baptizer.

Are you the kind of person who has to do something when you think about it or else you are likely to end up forgetting to do it? Perhaps the editor of the Gospel according to John was such a person: strike while the iron is hot; mention this idea while I am thinking of it. That appears to be what has happened in the first chapter of John.

The chapter opens with a beautiful, poetic account about the eternal Word. "In the beginning was the Word, and the Word was with God, and the Word was God." Then the lovely lines continue, flowing into language about light: "The light shines in the darkness, and the darkness did not overcome it."

All of a sudden, evidently this phrase reminds the evangelist of something that cannot wait, so in the middle of the elegant poetry comes a shift. We are given three quick verses (John 1:6-8) that just cannot be delayed, and then the writer goes back into the poetic mode, as if nothing has happened.

What was going on? Why did the writer/editor of this material stop so quickly and insert these three verses about John the Baptizer? In the early days of the church there had developed some vocal and active followers of John the Baptizer. They admired the work of John the Baptizer so much that they paid more mind to his story than they did to the account of the message of Christ. Even on into the first century of the church, these followers of the Baptizer were themselves rivals of those who followed Jesus. Some of them saw John the Baptizer as God's light in a world of darkness. (There is a small sect today in Iran and Iraq, Sabaean Mandeans, who still hold that view.)

So when the writer of John's Gospel account began writing about the light that shines in darkness, he thought, *Good grief, some folks will think that I mean that John the Baptizer is the light!* So, he stopped right in the middle of what he was doing and corrected that possible error. He said it gently, but he said it clearly: "There was a man sent from God, whose name was John. He came as a witness to testify to the light, so that all might believe through him. He himself was not the light, but he came to testify to the light." Thus, the writer of John sets the matter straight: don't confuse the one who points to the Light with the Light itself. Nor should I confuse the sign that says "Raleigh 23 miles" with being my state capital itself. The sign is not the same as the place. The one who points is not the same as that to which he points.

This is a lesson we would do well to remember. All around are signs and pointers that become confused with the Light. The celebration and tinsel and sparkle that we are packing away for another year reflect the joy at Christ's birth, but should not be confused with the Messiah. The effort to make our worship space distinctive, even beautiful, is a worthy task, but it should not be confused with the One whom we gather to worship. Our busyness and activity, even in good causes, should point to our Lord and not be a substitute for the Lord's presence.

How can the church point to Christ? We point to Christ when we show what he has done. Transformed lives. Persons living in peace. Sins forgiven. New beginnings accepted. Healing of broken bodies. *Murder in the Cathedral* is T. S. Eliot's dramatic description of the death of Archbishop Thomas Becket. Eliot writes that as the murderers moved in to complete their menacing work, the archbishop said to those who loved him: "I am not in any danger; I am only near to death." We point to Christ when we point to the saving work he has done among us.

How can the church point to Christ? We point to Christ when we see where he is already alive in ministry and then join him in that mission. John 1:18 notes, "No one has ever seen God. It is God the only Son, who is close to the Father's heart, who has made him known." We get to know God when we see the Christ in mission. That is one reason that Epiphany begins a season when the church habitually gives emphasis to the work of missions. (See "Have You Thought of Doing This?") God is at work all around us. God works in the church, but God also works in the home. God works in a flower shop and God works in a state legislature. God works in a science lab and God works in a prayer chapel. Maybe this is why Jesus said, "The kingdom of heaven has come near" (Matthew 10:7). Then Jesus follows with examples of how the disciples are to follow him in that kingdom mission: "cure the sick, raise the dead, cleanse the lepers, cast out demons." Kingdom work involves the interior and the exterior of our lives; kingdom work involves those whom society rejects and those forces that destroy from within. We point to Christ when we join him in such work.

The "bottom line" of the work of John the Baptizer was "that all might believe through him" (John 1:7). "All" suggests that there are no exceptions to God's invitation. The sovereign God has not picked some for belief and decided that others should not have that gift. Belief, as the word is used here, is not a head trip of accepting certain facts as true. Belief is reliance and trust and obedience. It is what the Wesleyan tradition means by sanctification as the evidence of justification. The mission of the Baptizer (and our mission) is measured by the "all-ness" of the mission and the "belief " of the all.

The one to whom we point is the Word: *Lŏgŏs*. "Logos" means speech, communication, a letter. Another way to put John 1:1 is to declare: When God had something to say, Jesus is what God said! John is clear that this Word is the same creative Word that brought all life into being (John 1:3). The Word is not a Johnny-come-lately. The Word is the eternal God (John 1:1).

In John 1:5, the Gospel writer uses the present tense and the past tense in the same sentence: "The light *shines* in the darkness, and the darkness *did not* overcome it" (emphasis added). Remember that John is writing after the risen Christ has been among the disciples, so he is probably pointing out that the Light of Christ still shines because in the death of Jesus, the Light was not overcome (literally, was not taken down). I am reminded of those trick birthday candles that one can blow out but they keep coming back to full flame. Jesus died, but the resurrection shows that "blowing out the candle" did not have the final word about the Word!

The mission of testifying to the Word is not easy. We are warned that already "the world did not know him" and that "his own people did not receive him." But then, "being the Word"— living the Word—is not easy. In fact, it is death, Jesus' death. Try to find a picture of the Crucifixion panel of the Isenheim Altarpiece by Matthias Grünewald. (You can use a search engine to locate it on the Internet.) The artist shows the absolute torture of the dying Savior. True to the technique of many of his contemporaries in the early sixteenth century, Grünewald shows Christ as physically much larger than others in the scene. That was a way to make clear who was the most important figure in the painting. The draining blood, the ill-colored flesh, the gaunt arms and anguished fingers all show the depths of "the world that received him not." Over the head of Jesus is the mocking sign "INRI"—Jesus of Nazareth, King of the Jews. Mary, the mother of Jesus, has collapsed into the arms of John, the Evangelist. Mary Magdalene is crushed with her grief. This is death at its most gruesome. But to the side, also at the foot of the cross, stands John the Baptizer. Grünewald shows the Baptizer with a bony hand, pointing to Christ on the cross. Even in death on the cross, Jesus is the Light of the world, and the Baptizer still fulfills his mission: to point to the Savior.

In the biblical account, of course John the Baptizer died before Jesus did (Matthew 14:10), but the Grünewald painting was not intended to be a news report. It was intended to stir our passions to know that it is always, always time to point to Jesus.

Where do we see Jesus? This anonymous poem has circulated on the Internet:

I Saw Jesus

I saw Jesus last week.
He was wearing blue jeans and an old shirt.
He was up at the church building;
He was alone and working hard.
For just a minute he looked a little like one of our
church members.
But it was Jesus; I could tell by his smile.

I saw Jesus last Sunday.
He was teaching a Bible class.
He didn't talk real loud or use long words,
But you could tell he believed what he said.
For just a minute, he looked like my Sunday school teacher.
But it was Jesus; I could tell by his loving voice.

I saw Jesus yesterday.
He was at the hospital visiting a friend who was sick.
They prayed together quietly.
For just a minute he looked like our pastor.
But it was Jesus; I could tell by the tears in his eyes.

I saw Jesus this morning.
He was in my kitchen making my breakfast.
He then fixed me a special lunch to take with me.
For just a minute he looked like my mom
But it was Jesus; I could feel the love from his heart.

I saw Jesus today.
He was praying on his knees, all alone.
He then began to cry for those he prayed for.

For just a minute he looked like a lady from our church.
But it was Jesus; I could see the compassion
poured out of his prayer.

I saw Jesus the other day.
He was at the grocery store talking to friends.
He then put his arms around them to comfort them.
For just a minute he looked like a
young mother in our ladies class.
But it was Jesus; I could see the concern for others who hurt.

I see Jesus everywhere,
Taking food to the sick,
Welcoming others to his home,
Being friendly to a newcomer
And for just a minute I think he's someone I know.
But it's always Jesus; I can tell by the way he serves.

A Time with Young Disciples

Have the word "Epiphany" written in large letters on a big
piece of paper. Hold up the paper and ask the children how to
pronounce the word. (Some may know. Some may guess. Some
can't read. Some couldn't care less. You know—the usual mix.)

Make sure that someone (even if it's you!) has pronounced it
correctly: e-PIFF-a-nee. Say that this word means "appearance"
or "showing forth," the kind of thing that happens when you see
something you had not seen before or when you understand
something you had not understood before. That is an epiphany.
It is what some folks call "an aha moment," when suddenly you
say, "Oh, now I get it!"

Sometimes the church celebrates Epiphany as a way of saying
"Aha! Now I get it. When the wise men came to see the child
Jesus, it meant that Jesus was for everybody, all kinds of people,
Gentiles as well as Jews, folks from close by, such as the shep-
herds, and folks from far away, such as the wise men."

Today in this service we shall speak about another Epiphany.
(As a reminder, ask again: "Now, what does the word mean?"
Don't hesitate to give a clue if the children seem to have dozed

off earlier when you were being brilliant.) Another Epiphany. Another way of pointing to who Jesus was. Another "showing forth." Today we are going to talk about how John the Baptizer pointed people to Jesus. He showed people who Jesus was. His goal was for people to say, "Aha! Now I know who Jesus is and now I know what Jesus does and now I want to follow Jesus!"

(If you have a brave soul who would like to tackle the assignment, ask him or her to dress up like John the Baptizer. Somewhere along in here during the Time with Young Disciples, "John" makes an appearance. A wig, a bathrobe, and a honeycomb ought to complete the look.)

Talk about John seemed to touch on how he dressed funny and how he did not always act like other people. (Does your actor/actress look strange?) But God used John the Baptizer to help people get ready for Jesus, so when Jesus arrived on the scene, John could point at Jesus and everyone would know who it was. John was clear on one thing; his job was to show people Jesus.

How do we show people Jesus? John did it a lot by talking about Jesus, but we can point people to Jesus also by the way we live, the way we help others, and the way we enjoy life with God's people at church.

Epiphany. Showing people Jesus. Aha!

Hymns

There are several Epiphany hymns about the three wise men (or six wise men or two wise men—the Bible does not really say how many there were). But there are not many hymns about John the Baptizer. Most of the hymns that mention John are about the baptism of Jesus.

Because of that, more fittingly this would be a good Sunday to use hymns that speak of the light. John 1:1-14 uses the word "light" six times, so the theme of light is clearly a part of the text for this service. If you have someone who plays music before and after the service (sometimes called prelude and postlude, or voluntary or praise music), encourage her or him to choose music that has "light" in its title or subject. (These selections could include "Light of the World, We Hail Thee"; "Christ, Whose Glory Fills the Skies"; "I Want to Walk as a Child of the Light"; "O Morning Star, How Fair and Bright"; "Break Forth, O Beauteous Heavenly Light"; "You Are the Light of the World"; "Shine, Jesus, Shine"; and "I Am the Light of the World.")

If you do decide to sing the traditional Epiphany hymn "We Three Kings," try it this way. Divide the congregation into two groups (left side and right side would work—that's probably better than saying "liberals on one side and conservatives on the other!"). Let the two sides sing the phrases alternately and then all join on the refrain.

For example:

Side One: We three kings of Orient are;
Side Two: Bearing gifts we traverse afar,
Side One: Field and fountain, moor and mountain,
Side Two: Following yonder star
All: O star of wonder, star of light, star with royal beauty bright, westward leading, still proceeding, guide us to thy perfect light.

Repeat this for the other stanzas. Only in stanza four will this alternating singing violate the rules of punctuation. If you spot the problem and it doesn't bother you, I assure you it does not bother me. On the other hand, if you do not spot the problem, you shouldn't worry about that either!

Advent Wreath

The wreath is no doubt stored for another year. Consider putting a giant star in its place. (The star can stand high at the top of a stick. The star can be made of wood, foil, or pure gold. If it is made of pure gold, I'd like to talk with you about some favorite mission projects of mine.) The litany could be used if you have the star. Shine a floodlight on the star as the reading begins.

One Voice: The light of the world has come.
All Voices: Thanks be to God for the light.
One Voice: The light of a star has led to Bethlehem.
All Voices: Thanks be to God for the light.
One Voice: The light shines even in dark places.
All Voices: Thanks be to God for the light.

Have You Thought of Doing This?

This service reminds believers that to point to Christ is to identify places where Christ is at work and to join him in that work. What about local projects? What about mission teams to other places? What about trips to serve beyond national borders? What about efforts to support good legislation? What about a witness in solidarity with the rejected of society?

You never know how God will use mission in God's name. Several years ago, the church where I was pastor and another local congregation sent a work team to help build a church building in Dalvey, St. Thomas, Jamaica. The village housing consisted mostly of frail shacks, but they wanted a church that represented the centrality of God in their lives, a building that would honor the Creator of that place of beautiful land and sea. We worked on the foundation. Later teams put up walls. A final team added the strong roof. Within two years after the building was completed, a major hurricane sliced through the Caribbean. The entire village gathered in the church for safety and when they came out to inspect the damage, they found that only the church building had survived. The community lived there for weeks. That is something I never expected two years earlier when I hauled cinder blocks. Thank you, Lord.

Many denominations have national (and regional) offices that can direct you to places of mission and service. There are also ecumenical and nondenominational resources. Obviously, this list is a sampler. You can use your own contacts to find a mission that matches the call you are feeling from God. Remember that dollars sometimes minister where feet cannot go and feet sometimes minister in ways that dollars cannot.

Here are some ways to contact denominational and ecumenical mission and helping agencies.

American Baptist Church
www.nationalmissions.org
Post Office Box 851, Valley Forge, Pennsylvania 19482

Church World Service
www.churchworldservice.org
Post Office Box 968, Elkhart, Indiana 46515

Episcopal Relief and Development
www.er-d.org
815 Second Avenue, New York, New York 10017

Evangelical Lutheran Church in America
www.elca.org (Our-Faith-In-Action)
8765 West Higgins Road, Chicago, Illinois 60631

Habitat for Humanity
www.habitat.org
121 Habitat Street, Americus, Georgia 31709

Heifer Project International
www.heifer.org
1 World Avenue, Little Rock, Arkansas 72202

Hinton Rural Life Center
www.hintoncenter.org
2330 Hinton Center Road, Hayesville, North Carolina 28904

Oklahoma Indian Missionary Conference
www.umc-oimc.org
3020 Harvey, Oklahoma City, Oklahoma 73109

Presbyterian Disaster Assistance
www.pcusa.org/pda
100 Witherspoon Street, Louisville, Kentucky 40202

Stop Hunger Now
www.stophungernow.org
2501 Clark Avenue, Suite 301, Raleigh, North Carolina 27607

United Church of Christ National Disaster Ministries
www.ucc.org/disaster
700 Prospect Avenue, Cleveland, Ohio 44115

United Methodist Committee on Relief
www.new.gbgm-umc.org/umcor
475 Riverside Drive, Room 330, New York, New York 10115

Seasonal Funerals

There is a special sadness upon entering a home where there has been a death and seeing a Christmas tree and under it perhaps presents for the deceased. The contrast between the joys of the season and the grief of loss is stark.

If there is to be a funeral at the church during Advent or the Christmas season, there is strength in leaving the worship space as it is for ongoing worship of God. To do so communicates that life and death are both part of an ongoing flow. In some traditions, the color of the paraments for services of death and resurrection is always changed to white, regardless of the season, a practice that in many Western cultures represents confidence in the resurrection. I do not argue with that custom. Another view is that the use of the seasonal color (purple or blue during Advent) signals that in the midst of death as in the midst of life, the church tells the saving story of Jesus. It is the same story that it was before the death occurred! You might discuss these options as you do service planning with the family.

Coming into a sanctuary with the season's signs around can make a difficult time even more difficult. Pastors often hear: "Jean just loved Christmas! It will be so hard to see all the reminders of Advent when I know she won't be here to enjoy them." Part of the healing can come in this setting in which loss is magnified. It is not made any easier because of its "theological rightness."

A homily during a service of death and resurrection might note the disparity between the season's brightness and the occasion's shadows. "Few of us would expect to be here on these days just following Christmas, a time of loss in the midst of a time of gifts, a place of loneliness in the midst of a place of joy, a people in change in the midst of a people of tradition. Yet, being here at this time and place and with these people tells again about Bethlehem, a place of birth, a time of new beginning, a people of hope. Maybe this *is* a good time to be here, reminded who we are simply by being where we are."

The seasonal texts can help focus the homily. John 7:25-31 offers a perspective that there are times when we wonder about the readiness or ability of Jesus to be the Messiah, to be God's anointed. Some of the crowd in this text certainly wondered about it. But our Lord says that folks should remember that the One who sent him is true. And it is a truth that we can trust, even in the center of life's uncertainties. John 1:1-14 speaks of the Word living among us, a comfort indeed when we feel so very alone. Sometimes a death comes as relief, particularly when a loved one has suffered over a long period. Isaiah 55:1 is an invitation from God for the thirsty to come and drink of good water. The dying days of a loved one is indeed like a parched life, longing to be refreshed. In death, God has invited the loved one to drink fully and freely. Matthew 2:13-23's shocking version shows that death may think it can win against God, as Herod swoops in and brings the power of death. But Mary, Joseph, and the child are delivered, and the very one Death wanted to kill has lived. Does this service of death and resurrection let Death know that it has not won?

If a funeral is held in a place other than a congregation's worship space, the seasonal emotions may not be as near the surface. Even so, it is healthy for the pastor to pray in ways that acknowledge the seasonal context of the service. The prayer might be:

> Merciful God, who gave us the miracle of new life in Bethlehem, we thank you for the new life you give now to (*Name*). Our journey during Advent days has brought us with expectancy to the Holy Day of Jesus' birth. We bring to you that same anticipation and that same hope to this day and ask now that you bless it with a peace that the world cannot give and that, thanks be to your name, the world cannot take away.

In our ears rings a story of wise men, of shepherds, of new parents, and of a baby. Move our ears now to hear of a cross and an empty tomb, a cross that can save us and an empty tomb that points us toward a good tomorrow. We thank you for the way in which the life of (*Name*) has crossed our paths, and we rejoice that now (*his*) (*her*) path crosses the way with the Lord Jesus.

One of the hardest funerals I have conducted was for a long-time friend whose burial was on December 26. One of her daughters helped put the situation into perspective: "Mama would be glad to know that her funeral came at a time when everyone was still talking about Jesus."